# Making Lemonade

*An Antidote to the Existential Crisis*

by
Jade Miller

# Love Bites

## (Testimonials)

*An utterly refreshing, nourishing, and uplifting read for anyone in search of clarity, connection and creativity in work and life. In a wildly unconventional style Jade is unafraid to share her story, her battle scars, and her hard-won secrets for living a life on purpose. We're all better for it! 5 stars!*

—Mykel Dixon
Award-Winning Speaker, Experience Designer and
Author of *Everyday Creative*

*Written with humour and filled with practical advice, Making Lemonade had me hooked from the first page. Jade Miller demonstrates how, when life throws buckets of lemons, we gain insight into what is most important, so we start to live the life we truly want. Don't go wandering through life wallowing in the challenging circumstances! This is the book for you. Grab your copy today.*

—Mel Kettle
Leadership Communication Specialist, and
best-selling author of *Fully Connected*

*Quench your thirst here! In a world full of gurus telling you what to do from an ivory tower, Making Lemonade is a refreshing, pragmatic and relatable guide. Jade's care, wisdom and generosity is only surpassed by some bloody great advice, providing compelling and actionable ways to make sweet with the sour.*

—Kate Crawshaw
Chief Experience Officer (and navel gazer) Serious Woo

*"There aren't many books that make you smile and nod in agreement from the first page, but this one does. In this book Jade Miller shares her wonderful insights, quirky sense of humour and creative activities that encourage you gently, kindly and compassionately to use all the magnificent lemons we get given, to help us make better sense of the absurdities we call life.*

*No one is perfect, thank goodness. We are all unique, fallible and prone to stuffing things up in spectacular fashion. Jade reminds us, this is OK. It doesn't matter one jot what diagnosis you have been given or have given yourself. What really matters is working out what your preferences and strengths are so you can use them wisely, your priorities to avoid getting sucked down the plughole of life's complexities and your thinking patterns that can set you up to believe everything is S.H.I.T when in reality it's merely another asteroid belt of big juicy lemons that will make the best tasting lemonade ever."*

—Dr Jenny Brockis
Lifestyle Medicine Physician, Workplace Health and Wellbeing Consultant,
Best Selling Author and Award Winning Speaker

*"Jade's way of talking is funny and light, but when she gets deep, it's like a switch flips. She makes you think and gives you things to do that really hit you in the feels. And her drawings? They're like the icing on the cake, making the whole journey into Jade's world both smart and smile-worthy."*

—Rauhena Chase
Founder Rauhena Chase Commercial Real Estate

*"The juice is always worth the squeeze, but how do you squeeze it in a way that feels just right for you? In Making Lemonade, Jade's personal anecdotes, experiences, and ideas will keep you engaged and uplifted, as she guides you on a journey of pragmatic self-discovery and growth. She keeps it real and so accessible, you'll be thirsty for more!"*

—Leanne Hughes
Author: *The 2-Hour Workshop Blueprint*,
Keynote Speaker and Consultant

*"Making Lemonade is honest and vulnerable and reads like you're hanging out with a great friend. The real perspective and honesty that Jade shares in this book is so refreshing. She doesn't hold back in sharing her challenges which makes it so relatable and there are tangible, actionable steps to help you turn what life throws you into lemonade!"*

—Deanne Gagnon
Podcast Host - Workplaces that Work

*"This is raw and honest and a real gem to read. I congratulate the author for sharing her experiences to help others. Very enjoyable and some interesting insights into the neuro spicy world."*

—Theresa Davies
HR Consultant

Making Lemonade
An antidote to the existential crisis:

First published in 2024 by Jade Miller in Meanjin (Brisbane) Australia.

The author would like to acknowledge the traditional custodians of the land on which this book was written, paying respect to elders past and present of the Jagera people and the Turrbal people.

Copyright © 2024 by Jade Miller

The moral rights of the author have been asserted.

All rights reserved.

Book Cover and Formatting provided by Trisha Fuentes

Illustrations and cover design by Jade Miller

No part of this book may be reproduced in any form or by any electronic or mechanical means, including information storage and retrieval systems, without written permission from the author, except for the use of brief quotations in a book review.

The content presented in this book is meant for inspiration and informational purposes, and is not intended as a substitute for the advice from professionals. The author and publisher claim no responsibility to any person or entity for liability, loss or damage caused or alleged to be caused directly or indirectly as a result of the use, application or interpretation of the material in this book.

Every reasonable effort has been made to reference inspiration or content from other sources. The author welcomes information leading to more complete acknowledgement for future printings.

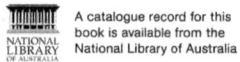
A catalogue record for this book is available from the National Library of Australia

ISBN: 978-0-6486204-0-2 (Paperback)
978-0-6486204-1-0 (Ebook)
978-0-6486204-2-6 (Audiobook)

*~ To my gorgeous daughters, you keep me going in this crazy world. ~*

# Contents

**About the Author** ........................................................ 1
**Introduction** ............................................................. 3

**PART 1 - YOURSELF** .................................................. 12
   Introduction - Driving the Car ................................... 13
   2 - Being with Yourself ............................................ 17
   3 - Understanding the 3 Ps ....................................... 25
   4 - Defining your PREFERENCES ................................ 29
   5 - Setting your PRIORITIES ...................................... 39
   6 - Recognising your PATTERNS ................................. 53
   7 - Checking your Mental Health ................................. 71
   8 - Taking Personal Responsibility .............................. 79

**PART 2 - OTHERS** ..................................................... 88
   Introduction - Connecting with Others ......................... 89
   10 - Feeling Disconnected ........................................ 95
   11 - ACCEPTANCE of Self ......................................... 105
   12 - NON-JUDGMENT of Others ................................. 109
   13 - COMPASSION for People .................................... 115
   14 - HONESTY is the Best Policy ................................ 119
   15 - OPENNESS with Others ..................................... 123
   16 - RELATIONSHIPS for a Connected Life .................... 127
   17 - Showing Up .................................................... 131
   18 - Balancing the Buckets ....................................... 141

**PART 3 - LIFE** .................................................. **148**
   Introduction - Life, Absurd Life ..............................149
   20 - Exploring Purpose.........................................153
   21 - Living the Millennial Middle-Class Dream................159
   22 - Looking at Social Constructs ...........................169
   23 - Challenging Systems and the Bureaucracy..............177
   24 - Comparing, Contrasting, Critically thinking..............183
   25 - Feeling the Disproportionate BS........................191
   26 - The Meaning Matrix......................................199
   27 - Embracing Life ........................................... 211
**Acknowledgements** ..........................................**215**
**Ways to work with Jade** .....................................**217**

# About the Author

Jade is obsessed with understanding humans and connecting authentically with people. Skilled in visual thinking, strategic problem solving and coaching, Jade uses her passion for communication and creativity to help others find their own sense of purpose. Being an autistic ADHD'er, with a special hyperfocus interest in psychology, sociology, culture and relationships, this shines through as her work as a communicator and artist who helps businesses and individuals develop strategy and vision for purposeful contribution.

Having overcome huge life challenges including neurosurgery, chronic illness, divorce, and her late diagnosis of Autism and ADHD, she is navigating life and business, keeping it real with a quirky sense of existential humour.

Jade has 20 years of experience in communication, marketing and design across a broad range of disciplines, and a lifetime of autistic hyper-interests and creative pursuits. She has appeared on several business podcasts including Ways to Change the Workplace, The Brand Called You, Six Comms, and The Craft of Consulting to talk about visual communication, clarity and connection, and she regularly shares visuals, thoughts and information on LinkedIn.

Jade lives in beautiful Brisbane, Australia with her two daughters and you will often find her spending time with them at the beach, or painting abstract art. She truly believes that life is about connection with ourselves and each other and finding ways to fill our lives with things we love doing.

# Introduction

Have you ever felt like life didn't really turn out how you thought it would? Like an 'expectations vs reality' meme, but it's not on the internet, you're living it. Existence threw you a mixed bag of lollies... or more like a mixed bag of sour citrus. Good times, accompanied by those nasty lows, new scenarios to deal with every week, sometimes really big and challenging events. Has it left you wondering how to make sense of it all? Yeah, me too.

This book is for anyone who's ever faced the paradoxes of life, sought meaning amidst the chaos, connection in isolation, and laughter in unexpected places. It's a book about making the best out of this crazy life, through understanding ourselves, building connection and finding meaning in the absurdity. Lemons all around? Well, all we can do is get about making that lemonade.

If you haven't already, be sure to visit [www.making-lemonade.com.au/workbook](www.making-lemonade.com.au/workbook) to download your free workbook. It has bonus material and plenty more space for scribbles and insights as you meander through these pages.

You'll also notice some song lyrics around the place. I've created a Spotify Playlist called 'Making Lemonade with Jade Miller'. If you search for it, you can listen along while you're reading.

Many moons ago I was sitting at a reception desk for my receptionist job - working full time for a record label. All day I greeted musicians and music industry people, while doing mundane admin-type tasks, but I loved it. Three evenings a week I was hosting a rock music TV show, curating playlists of up-and-coming bands, as well as older rock favourites. Most evenings I was going to gigs and partying. In many ways I was living my best life, in other ways it was a totally destructive period (free tickets to any gig I wanted was a dangerous perk). Anyhow, as I tapped away doing my work, not long before my 23rd birthday, it occurred to me that maybe one day I would write a book. I didn't know what on earth I thought I'd write about at 22, dismissed as quickly as it appeared, it joined a vault of 'impossible dreams' in my mind. But life, as it does, moved forward in unpredictable ways.

Fast forward, a lot of things happened in between then and now. One day, in the height of illness at age 38, it all just started pouring out of me. All the things I'd endured, all the things I was waking up to, all the things I'd learned just tumbled out onto pages.

Somewhere amongst the oodles of raw words, that memory re-occurred to me, and I realised that maybe I would actually write the book. I have grappled with my ingrained low self-worth, come and gone from this project several times through the last few years, but finally it's done. I bloody well did it. A bit for me, but mostly for you. You, the one who tussles with life, manages way more than your plate can hold, and figures there is more to existence than the daily hum drum. It's for you, resilient but a bit tired, disconnected yet attached, in malaise yet hopeful. (OK, this is really for me too.)

I don't really know how this has happened. I'm a working single mum with chronic health issues and a terrible phone addiction. But I am a spicy-brained woman with autism and ADHD, so I do have that benefit of hyperfocus. I've spent weekends and nights pulling words out of my soul, agonising over design, wondering if any of it is worth it. But if just one person can feel seen, accepted, and inspired reading these rough and ready chapters, then I'll be happy.

I've had a constant internal voice named Janice through this process, who keeps reminding me that there are plenty of books in the world, loads of self-help guides, a lot of Instagram inspiration, and why would I want to add more noise? She constantly questioned the value of adding my voice to the crowded space of self-help narratives. Who am I to write a book? Well, I guess it emerged from those spontaneous outpourings, a commitment to perseverance, a challenge to my own self-doubt, and a celebration of the unique lens through which my neurodivergence allows me to view the world.

If you're holding this in your hand right now, I want to say THANK YOU. I hope you make it past the first section.

Really though, I do hope that you find something that you can relate to. I hope that you discover something new about yourself as you ponder the stories, tools and creative activities.

I hope you agree, question and disagree with things in here.
I hope you can laugh at my quirky sense of humour.

I hope you embrace creativity in your life.
I hope you find more connection and purpose.
I hope you tell someone about it.

Life gets hard, and sometimes we get a bit lost.
We have so many pressures.
Financial
Family
Work
Health
The world!

It's a lot. But there is still space for love, healing and compassion. And that's ultimately what this book is for.

An antidote to our collective existential crisis. A guide to finding connection in our hard times. A way to uncover personal purpose.

Now that I've set you all up for rainbows and ice cream, I need to tell you the flavour you'll get here isn't always super sweet. Because is life? I'm an optimistic nihilist, seeing the beauty in the darkness, and the darkness in existence.

I've had my fair share of lemons, some of which have been completely outside my control. For example, there was this house I lived in that had a huntsman spider plague. I'm not remotely kidding. As an arachnophobe, it was literally living a nightmare. It started off with one or two, quite large hairy spiders visit the apartment. Not unusual in Queensland. Not my favourite thing, but understandable. It turned into so many giant spiders in my living space most weeks. They were in my bathroom, on my chairs, walking up the stairs, in my art supplies, on my bedside table, and even in my bed. I was BESIDE MYSELF. I never knew when one would appear, there was even one crawling on me, in the car, at nighttime. My nervous system was an absolute wreck, and I tried all kinds of tricks including home remedies and pest control, but FYI, nothing can get rid of a huntsman invasion except…a flood. That's right, a year and a half of dealing with these spiders, then a huge flood happened in Brisbane, and the bottom floor of my unit was washed out. It was awful, I lost a lot of belongings and then I had to move. That's what I'd call a fat juicy lemon right in the eye. But to make it sweet… at least I don't have a spider plague in my new place?

Lemons will come. Whether they're placed nicely at the doorstep, or pelted at you from across the street, they will come. However I want this book to feel like a warm hug. I want you to read it as if I am kind a Aunty who has some good tricks up her sleeve for getting through life.

There are many sour and upsetting things. Humans can be really shit, with their greed, and their hierarchies and competitive violence. There will always be those with more, and those with less. Equality is not actually attainable, and we're too far gone with climate change… BUT humans can be absolutely incredible too. With generosity and grace, modern inventions and healing…we can get mad at the world, but it doesn't serve anyone to stay in a place of anger.

The reality is that humans have always been this way but maybe, just maybe, there's a chance for more. More love, kindness, connection, self expression, contentment and resilience.

I know, it's hard. Especially if you're going through something that is particularly difficult and it just seems so unfair.

So, I've put some words together, and I hope they help you. I hope you find some connection to yourself and others, self-compassion, laughter and a sense of purpose through your inevitable challenges.

*I hope you feel less alone, and more yourself.*

As a neurodivergent person, when growing up, my behaviours and communication were a bit different to many people around me. Sometimes my schtick just didn't land, and I'd be teased and laughed at, yelled at, or isolated. So, I observed responses and reactions, and I started to learn how to communicate more effectively. I excelled in English, social studies, the arts, and was innately a very creative and expressive kid, growing into a highly attuned adult.

DISCLAIMER: I am not a psychologist, but I have a fixation and special interest in psychology and sociology and have keenly observed the humans in my life, on TV, media, and around me. I've experienced so many different life scenarios and done A LOT of therapy. Does this qualify me to write a book? I don't know, but here I am!

Whether it resonates here or not, I'm coming to this project with love, wanting to discuss ideas, let people know they aren't alone in their hard times, and offer some tools that have helped me through mine. I might start to rant because of my bleeding heart, depressive with my... depression, but also hopeful with the glimmers of goodness that are always there if you look hard enough.

I figure there are a lot of other people who have invented things that many people subscribe to. Religion? Ethics? Capitalism? Psychology? Democracy? Autocracy? Education? Medicine? Consulting? The public service? PYRAMID SCHEMES!? ... All just made-up stuff. All these systems humans live by are created by humans, and adopted by humans, because we desire knowledge, structure and progress. We need to feel safe with our sets of rules. We constantly quibble about who's rules are the most right, and it divides nations on a daily basis.

The human quest for truth and control will never cease, so why not join in the conversation. Maybe there actually isn't any truth. Or there are 1000 truths. Perhaps there are even eight billion truths. I guess what I'm sharing here is my own truths about how I exist in this blue sphere that is floating in an eternity of darkness. I'd like to encourage others to observe their own version.

The other thing I want to acknowledge, is that I hold a certain level of privilege as an educated white woman. Not really any more privileged than most people I know. I put myself through university, I work hard, and I don't hold hope that I'll ever be able buy a house, but I feel privileged and lucky to have been born in New Zealand, live in Australia, and have reasonable security. However, my story is one with pretty big challenges, as I'm sure yours is too. A wise young guy I knew once, said to me, "The hardest thing YOU'VE been through, is the hardest thing YOU have been through." He meant that mostly, our challenges are relative to ourselves. They are subjective each to our own experiences. And it's in this spirit that I bring this to you. With compassion towards all the challenges we face, acknowledgment of all the ways we fall short, and all the ways we can shine.

The first part of this book is about YOURSELF. It's a little journey of self-discovery. An adventure into your soul and psyche to become more conscious of who you are. I truly believe this is the foundation for finding a sense of purpose, and making any changes that we want to. So often we can lose a sense of ourselves, be disconnected from what we truly value, and be blind to our faults. This section will help you understand, accept and look after yourself as a platform of strength to build from.

The second section is about OTHERS. How do we connect with people? How do we understand the wild wacky beings around us? We are disconnected from one another, and it is diminishing our experience of life. Relationships play a big role in discovering purpose, so we can always be getting better at them. Compassion and curiosity are a good place to start from, and if we've done the work within ourselves, it's much easier to step into that space.

Then we move into the big picture thinking about LIFE. What absurdity is this?! All these systems, processes, societal expectations, cultural rules… where do we find meaning amongst the madness?

With all my intent laid out for you to see, let's get to the guts of the book. Let's work together to make it so there are more humans BEING, and less humans just DOING. With an open heart and a mind attuned to both the challenges and triumphs of the human experience, let's navigate the inevitable lemons life throws our way with grace, resilience and a healthy dose of humor.

# PART 1 - YOURSELF

# 1

## Part 1 Introduction - Driving the Car

*"Where is my mind?"*

—Pixies

This part is all about YOU. You wild, crazy, interesting, precious human.

You are the main character in the story that is your life. What kind of lead role do you want to play? Is this something you've even thought about?

Well, here it is, YOU are the head honcho.

You get to choose what to do with what's been given to you.

You hold the keys to the car.

Will you get into the passenger's seat and hand them over to some other ghost of your past, or will you jump in the driver's seat, and put the other voices in the passenger seat?

Sometimes we avoid even looking at ourselves, because it can be quite painful to address those things about ourselves that we have tucked away in the darkness. But it's essential work. If we want to live a fulfilled life, understanding yourself is the foundation.

This 'self-discovery' section is not just 'woo-woo.' It isn't psychotherapy either. It's just what I've come to realise is an essential part of existing as human if you want to be effective in your work, your relationships, your life. To be honest, I've probably gone overkill on my own 'self-awareness' and overthink everything I do, but I've found it extremely helpful to move forward and navigate some hectic challenges.

There are a dozen ways to approach self-improvement. I mean, literally thousands of books have been written on this subject for many centuries. You'd think we'd be better at life with all this analysis, but if someone had figured out that there was just one way to go about it, we'd all be content and happy, and nobody would need to write anything more. But we are complex creatures. Not only are we individually unique, so are our circumstances. So, there are millions of ways to get through life. We're doing it all the time. What I have discovered has worked for me in some way, will not be everyone's cup of tea, but it might just help someone.

Circumstances are going to be hard. Life is going to be hard. How you manage and deal with that is what your happiness and contentment rely on. You. Your strength in adversity.

I have had a bad habit of slipping into blame and suffering sometimes.

Depression doesn't help me with breaking these cycles, but it also doesn't stop me from trying my best.

Whatever lead role you are choosing to play in your story, YOU, must learn to:

- Be aware of yourself;
- Accept and like yourself; and,
- Manage yourself.

WHY? Because if you'd like to enjoy your relationships, work, family, and existence more, if you'd like to handle the inevitable challenges that life is throwing at you, you really need this foundation of self-work. It will give you a solid platform to deal with anything that comes.

Oooh and geez the work is hard, and it's always in progress, so you never really arrive.

It means having a look in the mirror. Every damn day.
Reflect on how the day was.
How did you feel?
How do you think other people felt in relation to your behaviour and actions?
Why do you think that is?
Is this something that happens often?

It's time to get curious. Curious about how you respond to situations, how you talk to yourself, and how you present yourself in the world.

We often have a really nasty internal monologue that drives our decisions and behaviours without us even thinking about it, and these responses to people around us and situations that happen will build over time, whether they are positive or negative.

You can't expect others to understand you, if you don't really understand yourself.

We allow external forces to shape who we are, by passively consuming messages, without putting them through a critical thinking filter.

When we examine our responses and choices, we step closer to being the most accurate version of ourselves. When we ask ourselves 'why?' we give permission to own our own lives, find our truth and shape our lives to be aligned with what we really believe.

If there are things in your life you've been wanting to change, this is the best place to start. If there are challenges you are going through, that you don't have control over, this is where you get some control.

It all starts with you.

# 2

## Being with Yourself

*"It's me, hi, I'm the problem, it's me."*

—Taylor Swift

To start a journey of self-awareness, you must start with a bit of self-compassion.

My nasty internal monologue is a very shouty critical part of me, who I call Janice. I have to sideline her when I'm doing this work, because I'd bloody get nowhere otherwise. You can't be going through these sections, sharing your heart and ideas with nasty self-judgment and criticism. I have to call on the gentle, kind, compassionate part of me to support me while I do hard things. She's sometimes been completely overrun by Janice, and I've ignored and forgotten about her for some time. She's still there though, I just have to turn towards her and ask her to step up, while I tell Janice to pipe down.

Getting to know all your parts, and the REAL YOU are foundational to building resilience, becoming a better leader of your life, and moving through difficult situations.

Parts of this might be a bit uncomfortable, but you can't grow without discomfort. You might even want to get mad at yourself, that's normal. You might be a dick, and you don't even know it. I know I've been a real dick sometimes.

I'll have some good examples of that as I waffle on in here. Obviously, I'll talk about myself a bit, because that's how we roll when we're the author of the book. However, I want you to know this is a journey of self-discovery that we are all on together.

Acceptance of your feelings is massive in the path to self-awareness. Start to become more familiar with things that upset you and things that make you happy, feel the feelings that come up, and allow them. Allowing anger to exist, does not mean allowing the potential consequences of anger to play out, e.g., violence. But taking a breath when you have a big feeling, and asking yourself WHY you're feeling that way will help you understand and manage yourself in a much more functional and healthy way.

Examine feelings about situations, activities, relationships and gravitate in the right direction for your life. You might start to realise that there are things, people, situations in life that you need to address or let go of.

I have spent a lot of my life mostly misunderstanding who I am yet being acutely aware of my shortcomings. For example, I have always had this idea that I was terrible at sports. Because I wasn't super athletic at school, and I was surrounded by people who showed excellence in physical activities, I just didn't rate myself in that area, and nor did my peers. But as an adult, I've had comments on my ability for certain sporty skills, like, I can actually hit a ball for a game of tennis, and my pool skills can be pretty good. Especially after a couple of beers. I mean, my self-awareness wasn't too far off, I'm definitely not an athlete, but what I've realised is that I've been telling myself I'm terrible at something, where I'm actually not that bad. Even more importantly than that, I've been measuring my athleticism against some really high standard, and then beating myself up about not attaining it. This doesn't have a marathon running ending, but it's freed me up to play a bit of tennis and be more regular in moving my body. It's amazing how addressing even the seemingly innocuous negative perceptions can unlock something in your life.

## What don't you know about yourself?

Sometimes we don't find these things out until something drastic happens. Big situations will always bring out true parts of you. We see it with classic examples like Bridezillas in the wedding planning, or relatives at a will readings after a death. We all have that Johari Window quadrant of blindness, and always will. But the more we learn about ourselves, the smaller it gets.

**Johari Window:**

I would argue that 'self-awareness' is the underpinning foundation to getting anywhere you'd like to go in life. Self-awareness is the key success factor for personal growth. Awareness of your relationship to yourself, what your Achilles heels are, and the impact you have, will set you up for improvements in life.

We spend a lot of time chatting to ourselves. Our brains are creating all kinds of thoughts, and for some, even full-blown conversations. This does NOT mean you are 'crazy', it's pretty normal to have an internal dialogue. So, since there are so many opportunities to communicate with ourselves, we better try and make it quality, right?!

## ACTIVITY - Rewriting the Monologue

*We all have stories going on in our mind, about who we are and what our capabilities are. Write a little monologue to remind your brain about the things you're working towards, what you are going to accept, and how incredible you are doing. Often, we don't even realise that we're telling ourselves nasty things. Here is my little monologue, to try and reaffirm my goals, and counteract the shouty criticiser.*

*Get your head out of your phone. It's better for your brain.*
*Move your body. It's really good for your mental health and makes you feel alive.*
*Eat more vegetables. You're doing great.*
*Reach out to people. They enjoy hearing from you.*
*Nobody is bringing your future to you, you have to go and get it.*
*Cry on the couch, but get up and live again. You've got this.*
*You're super smart, fun and cool.*
*Yes, you're intense, some people won't (don't) like it. Just don't hang around them.*
*You are SO creative, loving and conscientious.*

*You're achieving a lot, be proud of yourself.*

*And when I deliver the goods, even small things like getting some groceries - which I find quite difficult some days - I have a chat to myself about how well I've done: Revisit these words you create to really drive the message home. Even memorise parts of it if you can. Don't be shy to start telling yourself you've done a good job, even on the smallest of tasks. Rewire your brain from loathing to love!*

MAKING LEMONADE

# MY NEW INTERNAL MONOLOGUE!

When we understand our own thoughts, feelings and behaviours we can make more informed choices about how we go about our day-to-day lives.

Knowing our own strengths helps move us towards things we can excel in and enjoy.

Conversely, understanding our limitations gives us an opportunity to avoid certain things, or to proactively learn and develop new skills.

So how do we understand ourselves more? Isn't that a bit self-centred and egotistical? Is it even worth it? Shouldn't people just accept me for how I am?

Well, yes, but also no. It's actually an important avenue for having a BETTER existence. A healthier relationship with ourselves leads to healthier connections, and greater understanding of the context that we live in.

What invisible clothing do we put on that serves a purpose, but stops us from being truly ourselves? What parts of ourselves have we hidden away in disgust, hoping to never have to deal with them again? Usually, we avoid looking in the mirror, like, really truly looking, because it's hard to accept these parts.

We're terrified of 'negative' emotions, and afraid to address behaviours that are problematic. Turning towards those parts of ourselves that we so strongly dislike is very uncomfortable. Fronting up to those parts of yourself that you've hidden away can be terrifying, so we go along without really knowing or being ourselves.

I don't like seeing my emerging wrinkles, let alone my emotional dysfunction.

Nevertheless, I commit to a life journey of self-examination, and the lesson is this:

*Those parts you try to run and hide from will always show up somewhere.*

Behaviours, emotions, and situations; you're probably letting some of those parts of you have control over your life and you don't even know it. There are parts of me I've discovered in more recent years that I didn't even know were there but have been crying out for my attention. Literally.

I have spent more than a few times sobbing in weird places.
Bathrooms and the kitchen floor, toilets in some random locations.
Buses and trains.
At my desk at work; hoping nobody sees me.

I'm not going to sugarcoat this self-investigating process, when you start poking around in the past, it could get messy on the kitchen floor. But I will say that it's worth it, and I would not have made it through as strong as I have, if I hadn't done this work in asking myself WHY I am the way I am. What happened to me? Who am I? Are aliens real?!

And then when I discover the answers, learning how to be with myself, accepting these parts and building a new foundation.

Now, this process can be as deep or as shallow as you want it to be, it's your journey. Skim over it, or delve in. It's totally up to you.

# 3

## Understanding the 3 Ps

*It's just me myself and I"*

—De La Soul

For me, soul searching began as a kid, trying so very hard to comprehend who I was, how I related to others, and what everything meant. I mean, what a way to start life. Such a deep little thinker with a very early sense of existential dread.

I went through my life observing people's reactions, made mental notes of patterns I saw, observed my own responses to things, and for the most part, decided that I was too different and that was dangerous. As a younger kid,

I would give my opinions, share my thoughts, yell out the answers in class and that wasn't always met with acceptance. People in my life got annoyed or angry with me, what I had to offer often wasn't welcomed, so the safest thing to do was tone it down. Perhaps that is the experience of many people.

I tried to hide me. I learned new ways of communicating. Mostly to keep quiet. The tricky thing about this process of masking and quietening your true self, is that it warps your personality. I was trying to escape the feelings of insecurity I had about myself, so at school I'd get myself into trouble. I gravitated towards the disruptors and was a bit disruptive myself. I got away with it mostly, because I was smart in my tiny rural New Zealand school. I tried to fit in, be cool, find social status, but never really could. I had conflicts with friends, and behaved quite wildly at times, getting into trouble for stealing, swearing, drinking, and being in places I wasn't supposed to.

I knew I had a different brain, but it's taken 40 years of exploring, and a societal movement towards openness about neurodivergence to find out exactly what kind.

Seeking to understand yourself doesn't come naturally to some people, in fact I think there are people who deliberately avoid getting to know themselves on a deeper level, because that might be a bit scary. Then there are others who revel in the self-improvement, with all their mindfulness and 4.30am ice baths. I like to try and sit somewhere in between; I feel like middle ground is healthy. A little bit of discovery, a little bit of leaving the past behind.

So, over those many years of struggling with social interaction, much therapy and self-development I've come to discover as an adult, that there are ways that we can learn more about ourselves. I've designed a framework that we can follow to start the process of discovering more of who we really are. 3 Ps. Yeah it's a little bit cheesy, but it's helpful to have a framework as we explore. Looking at our Preferences, Priorities and Patterns can give insight into what we really want, what demands our time and energy, and how we operate. Then we can identify potential areas for change. Or we have big realisations that we'll never achieve our dreams because priorities are too demanding. Either way, strap on in.

# 4

## *Defining your PREFERENCES*

*"I'm not scared to be seen
I make no apologies, this is me"*

**—The Greatest Showman**

I'm not going to take you through a long personality test here, we've all been there. It's likely you already have an idea of your attributes and what box you might fit into through some work team building thing you did. So that's a starting point. I will just go through what is generally understood as aspects of personality and pose some questions for you to consider.

However, if you haven't done a personality test, I do recommend doing some. They're pretty fun, and surprisingly insightful. My psychologist recommends Enneagram and Myers Briggs which are both quite popular, although they have been nicknamed as 'astrology for co-workers.'

The Enneagram model is based on the idea that there are nine basic personality types, each with a unique set of characteristics, strengths, and weaknesses. These types are identified by numbers ranging from one to nine, and each number represents a different way of seeing the world and responding to life's challenges.

The Myers-Briggs Type Indicator, which is based on Carl Jung's theory of personality is a self-guided questionnaire that assesses an individual's preferences across four dimensions: Extraversion/Introversion, Sensing/Intuition, Thinking/Feeling, and Judging/Perceiving.

The tests can provide a good indicator of the way you operate, but I don't think that any one of us can fit perfectly into one box. Humans are more complex and dynamic than we will probably ever understand, so giving yourself a four-letter label from the Myers Briggs might guide you, but it is not going to give you all the answers to life.

In case you're familiar with this stuff and wondering, I'm an ENFP but also strongly I. And I'm an Enneagram 4. (Generally, a crazy artist type.)

I'm not a psychologist, but I've (half) read many books, love doing personality tests, and I'm a keen observer of human behaviour. I'm still baffled by the unusual choices humans make on a daily basis - mostly when I see them driving a car - but if we can collectively become more aware of who we are, what choices we make and why, I'm sure we will all reach enlightenment in no time!

The first question to ask yourself is...

## What do you truly value?

Values speak about your motivations. Values are a key factor in your decision making and general sense of direction in life.

For some, living by their values is a high priority value, and for others, it sits much lower. Still, having a general understanding of the aspects of life that are most important to you, helps you to live more authentically, and reduces that internal struggle that can occur when we are participating in activities that don't align.

Understanding your own personal values isn't something we are necessarily directly taught. You glean an idea of what you like and don't like from your parents, but that doesn't always align with the person that YOU are, separate to them.

What is it you want? I ask myself this all the time. (Often the answer is to have a lie down.)

But seriously, what do you want, and why? Who do you (really) want to be?

It can take an entire lifetime to work this out. And by the time we feel like we know, we've probably changed, or we're on our deathbed. But let's have a go anyway.

MAKING LEMONADE

# ACTIVITY - What do you want out of life?

*Take a look at this list and tick the ones that resonate with you. What leaps out at you immediately? That's probably a really high value for you.*

- [ ] 1. *Authenticity*
- [ ] 2. *Compassion*
- [ ] 3. *Courage*
- [ ] 4. *Creativity*
- [ ] 5. *Curiosity*
- [ ] 6. *Dependability*
- [ ] 7. *Empathy*
- [ ] 8. *Fairness*
- [ ] 9. *Forgiveness*
- [ ] 10. *Gratitude*
- [ ] 11. *Simplicity*
- [ ] 12. *Honesty*
- [ ] 13. *Humility*
- [ ] 14. *Integrity*
- [ ] 15. *Kindness*
- [ ] 16. *Love*
- [ ] 17. *Open-mindedness*
- [ ] 18. *Direct communication*
- [ ] 19. *Patience*
- [ ] 20. *Perserverance*
- [ ] 21. *Respect*
- [ ] 22. *Responsibility*
- [ ] 23. *Self-discipline*
- [ ] 24. *Self-esteem*
- [ ] 25. *Self-expression*
- [ ] 26. *Self-reliance*
- [ ] 27. *Minimalism*
- [ ] 28. *Selflessness*
- [ ] 29. *Sensitivity*
- [ ] 30. *Service*
- [ ] 31. *Tolerance*
- [ ] 32. *Trust*
- [ ] 33. *Wisdom*
- [ ] 34. *Status*

*Here's a bit about my own values. Take some time to write something like this, about what you want in life.*

*I want an honest life.*
*I want genuine connections.*
*I want to explore and express my truest self.*
*I want to be comfortable in my resources, have treats and holidays, and freedom to choose what I do with my time.*
*I want to provide my children with as much as I can, more than I had.*
*I want to create a spacious home base where my loved ones feel free to be, to enjoy, to connect.*
*I want to share what I've learnt and encourage others to find a way of living that makes them happy and opens up their creative purpose.*
*I value people and their ability to choose.*
*I value the offering of choice and education.*
*I value love, connection, truth and honesty.*
*I love to address the elephants in the room.*
*I value trying our best, over actual results.*
*I value creative life, innovation, disruption, change, exploration, and ideas that improve the way of living for others.*
*I value equity, and growth, but not at the expense and exploitation of people and the planet.*

*These are things I strive to, and hope to do and be, but can't always 100% live by. It's sort of impossible to live exactly how you want. If we could, there'd be no tension, and for growth and purpose, there needs to be tension.*

# MY VALUES

## What's your temperament like, generally?

The next thing to consider when you're looking at what kind of personality you have is what you've possibly inherited through both nature and nurture.

These are the parts you've had no control over as a baby and child but have a huge impact on how you present in the world. There are likely characteristics of your parents that shine through sometimes, whether we like it or not.

Do you approach life with a laid-back attitude, or are you highly organised and driven. Are you anxious, or do you have a calm disposition?

Your temperament is kind of like your hardware, made up of varying degrees of energy, emotions, engagement, impulsiveness, sensitivity. (medlineplus.org)

PART 1 - YOURSELF

# ACTIVITY – What am I like?

*Use these sliding scales to think about your own temperament. Nominate where you might sit on each by marking a cross somewhere along the line.*

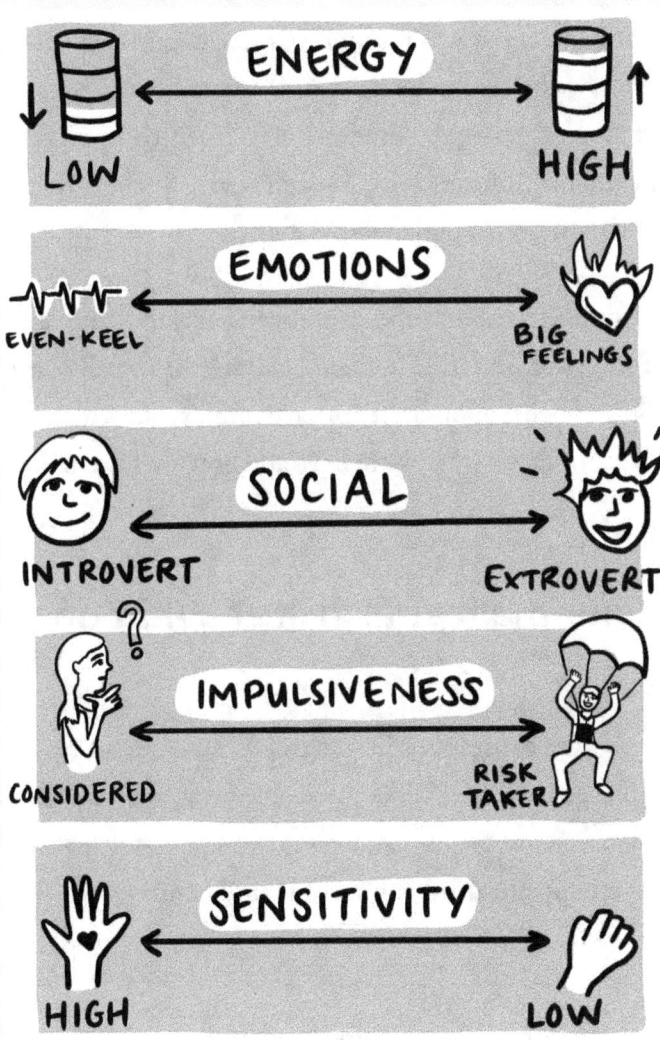

## What do you believe?

Remembering that beliefs can change, what are the foundations of your belief system?

We all have some kind of belief system going on. What we interpret about how the world works, how we respond to and categorise events of day-to-day life, and what we believe to be right and wrong. Some people have really defined belief systems that are based on prescribed things like a religious text, or political views. Others have a patchwork of beliefs that have been accumulated over life and experiences.

Sometimes we get stuck in an echo chamber of social media and think we believe something, but on reflection and analysis, we actually have our own deeper opinion and belief about it. It's often complex, but worth being mindful of. There is more about what we believe and how we find meaning in Part 3 - Life.

## What is your main goal in life? What do you WANT?

According to research giant Roy Morgan in 2013, people sit closer to one of the following five goals in life. What do you lean towards as a destination?

- Family - a happy healthy, connected family unit
- Security - financial and physical safety
- Prosperity - prosperity and wealth
- Excitement - adrenaline and adventure
- Importance - meaningful engagement with life

These goals can change, either by choice, or perhaps by force. Being forced to change goals can cause some struggle. For example, if you lean towards Excitement as a life goal, and you have a baby, things are going to change quite quickly and be very uncomfortable.

## Do you have any secret rules?

One of the things that I realised as part of my journey to discovering I am on the autism spectrum, is that I have a lot of secret rules. Things that have to be a certain way in order for me to function optimally. I have some really strong preferences, but for many years had hidden them and adapted as a coping mechanism. I believe this masking is what has caused anxiety and depression in my life, since I was a child.

The trouble with having both ADHD and being autistic, is that I love spontaneity, but crave order. I am chaotic but have very strong particularities.

Somewhere I learnt that being myself, with my own strong preferences wasn't safe or accepted, and I had to hide them. Maybe you're hiding some things too.

These secret rules I have are things like:

- I'm really particular about clothes and accessories that must go together. For example, I love the style of combat boots. But I can't own Doc Martens, because they have yellow stitching, and that yellow wouldn't go with everything in my wardrobe. It would annoy me too much.
- I dislike it when people driving stop randomly to let me cross the street as a pedestrian. Because it's too random. It's not the road rules. I don't like being rushed, I'd rather just make my own way, with the shared, normal rules, and cross the road when I feel it's safe.
- I can't eat a tomato without salt on it. And the salt HAS to be right on the tomato. It can't be generally on the sandwich, it must touch the tomato, because some kind of chemical reaction happens, and it optimises the flavour.
- I can't walk around the house without shoes or socks or slippers on, because the crumbs or dirt on my feet makes me CRAZY.
- I need to feel symmetry on my body. I can't wear totally odd socks.
- I need to be early, or at worst, right on time or I get super stressed.

OK, so you get the idea, I have a few quirks. What are yours? We can only figure out what these are by observing ourselves, and maybe other people point them out to us. What are your secret rules? Did you even know you had any?

So, there are a few questions to get you thinking about the preferences YOU hold as a human here. Sometimes we don't take the time to even think about it. We get so caught up in life's tasks that there's no opportunity to figure out how much we actually LIKE what we're doing, or how we're doing it.

# 5

## Setting your PRIORITIES

*"Tumble out of bed
And stumble to the kitchen
Pour myself a cup of ambition"*

—Dolly Parton

Priorities will ebb and flow in life. They shift and change depending on a range of factors. Your job, your friendships, relationships with family, care responsibilities, life.

Priorities are the tasks that change according to importance and urgency. Different pressures will influence what becomes priority. This day-to-day stuff that we deal with can be different every day. Yes, priorities are practical, but they are also connected to the intangible aspects of yourself that we discovered in our discussion about preferences.

There are external drivers in culture and society that can skew our sense of safety and push us towards prioritizing things that don't necessarily align with who we are and what is important for us.

The most obvious example to talk about is the huge shift in priority that happens when you have a child. Keeping a tiny human alive tends to promptly and aggressively change the way you operate. Well, at least it probably should.

Checking in about these is really important to know how YOU are going to approach your day, week, month…life…

## THE UNDERPINNING NEED FOR SAFETY

Firstly, I'd like to observe how I think as humans, we prioritise the safety of being part of the 'group.'

We are social creatures. At the core of our being it's important to maintain connection to 'the group.' It has been discussed that our primal nature seeks safety in numbers, in order to survive. I believe this is sort of an unconscious thing. It's like an innate instinct. There are two factors to consider when thinking about how safety influences our priorities:

1. Our own perceived position in our community. If our self-confidence and self-esteem is low, if we've been treated poorly as a child, if we really rely on external validation to feel secure, we likely have a view that we don't matter that much, and need to earn our way into the group.
2. The external influences that seek to jeopardise our perception of position within our community. The active voices that tell us how inadequate we are, through advertising and marketing, the media and politics, government, institutional religion.

They use a formula to influence (manipulate?) people into taking the actions they want them to.

The formula is:

***create a perceived threat, and then offer a promise to remove it.***

I think this happens deliberately and unintentionally through many facets of society, and in ways that we don't expect.

A classic example is the age-old way that the Christian church has hooked people in, is to scare people with the prospect of hell.

They present to you a threat. You will go to hell.

BUT here's the promise - if you accept Jesus as God, you'll be rescued from that impending doom.

I bought into this when I was in my early 20s and became part of a seriously dysfunctional church. Now, to be honest, I didn't really ever truly believe in hell, but it's sort of like a metaphor in life: Life is bad when you don't believe in (this thing). So believe in (this thing) and your life will be better. This is a formula many organisations employ, and in this case, it actually worked for me, for a short time.

The threat: A sad, lonely, sinful life.

The promise: Believe in Jesus and you'll get saved from that.

In this particular church community, there were a lot of criteria to what 'believing in Jesus' looked like. Publicly giving money to church, contributing to the community with a lot of time and energy, removing non-Christian relationships from your inner circle, prioritising being at church over everything else, OR you'd end up living out the threat - a sad, lonely sinful life.

Being manipulated in this way might seem silly on the outside. Many people don't understand how I ended up in this situation. I am pretty baffled when I look back, but I do know how it happened. I already felt like I was living the threat. I was lonely, confused, disconnected, with mental health challenges, substance issues, and searching for answers. I had left my home country and met up with a friend in a new city, who had found this great thing and she shared it with me. It made me feel connected, wanted, and my life actually genuinely got better.

At that time, it was the perfect solution for me. I cleaned up, felt more content, got a good job, made great friends, became more generous, forgiving, loving, and saw the world in a more positive way. Although there were some highlights about being part of a community, working towards good things, and believing in something, I then started to see faults very early on. So even though my genuine belief only lasted a short time, I still prioritised this, felt like I owed people, and that if I did leave, I would be outside 'the group'.

This was emphasised by the way leaders would talk negatively about anyone who had made a decision to leave the congregation. Somehow this threat of being outside the group allowed me to be manipulated into making this my number one priority. I let it take my time, my energy, and my sense of identity so that other things suffered. So, for what I might have gained, I also lost a lot. It was not a healthy space to be in, and it took a long time to understand, re-prioritise, and come out from that manipulative framework.

In my life, I've been through experiences like this many times. I follow threads of curiosity until it's been satiated, and really this was just a thread that lasted longer than I wanted it to. If I do end up in hell, well, see you there. Or not, because apparently it's lonely.

I'm pleased to say my life without this is actually going pretty well. I kept the good things, moved away from what I believed to be toxic, and now have great connections, and I feel fine about my 'sinful' activities. I sometimes wish I could still believe in that way, but that format is not for me. I admire those who have the diligence for prioritising a spiritual practice, and I met some of the most selfless and incredible people who gave a lot of time and resourcing to what they believe in. I've also met people who had all this in balance. Their spiritual beliefs are part of their priority list, but not taking up too much of it, and this is what I'm getting at.

We need to have a balanced approach and be conscious of what we are choosing to give energy to. There are things that will pull you in a certain direction, potentially not as extremely as this cult-like church example, but work might do it. Some jobs will take everything they can from you, leaving you with a sense that you won't be any good in another role, and causing other important things to drop off the list. Family might have high expectations of your time, with a mild threat of disconnection looming in the background, so you give more than you can manage, or make your life decisions based on their influence over you.

A common thing I see, and there's plenty of discussion around it - is the self-care aspect. Not bubble baths and the occasional massage, but giving your 'self' attention, asking it what it needs, and integrating life habits to ensure this is a real priority for YOU.

Misaligned priorities are the real danger, not being cast out of the 'group.' Do you really want to live a life based on someone else's idea of what you should be doing?

What are YOUR priorities, as aligned with your values and goals, and taking into consideration your current responsibilities?

Is something taking so much time, energy, resources that another priority is on the backburner, and you're suffering?

PART 1 - YOURSELF

Are you not enjoying things you used to enjoy, because they've overtaken your life - i.e., spending quality time with kids can be super hard if your tank is empty. You already know this stuff.

Is there any way to reconfigure things, so that you can bring what's important to YOU, further up the list?

## ACTIVITY - Priority Check

*Grab 2 different coloured highlighters and have a look at the lists of priorities on the next pages.*

*Sit in quiet for 2 minutes, thinking about 'What do I really want to focus on in my life'.*

1. *Use the first colour to highlight your top 5 personal priorities and 5 external priorities.*
2. *Use the second colour highlighter to highlight what you have done this week. Are there many crossovers? Are there totally different things highlighted? Are there many colour number 2 in your personal priority list? I hope so, and that this was a total waste of time, and you have everything in perfect balance!*

# PERSONAL PRIORITIES

- Personal hygiene
- Self-care activities
- Healing and personal work
- Social and recreational activities
- Religious or spiritual practices
- Personal creative projects or hobbies
- Exercise and physical activity
- Healthy eating and nutrition
- Sleep and rest
- Learning and education
- Career or life goals

PART 1 - YOURSELF

# EXTERNAL PRIORITIES

- Maintain immediate and extended family connections
- Work responsibilities
- Friend relationships and social interactions
- Digital life
- Financial management and budgeting
- Housekeeping and home organization
- Volunteering and community involvement
- Logistics for social events, holidays or extra-curricular activities
- School administration and commitments

47

These lists highlight that there are just as many personal priorities as there are external, but our to-do lists are often made up of the external things. The tendency to prioritise what's on the external list is because it's easier to do all these things, than to spend time looking at, and looking after, ourselves.

It's hard to look in the mirror and love ourselves. We're kind of conditioned to see what's wrong with ourselves, deeming ourselves unworthy of priority. Whether by childhood trauma and the people around us, or media and advertising or the systems we're forced to engage with, our sense of self-worth is compromised and diminished, and all these things we're supposed to do to elevate our wellbeing go by the wayside.

Women especially, take on so many of the external priorities, often automatically, because apparently our brains are good at holding multiple priorities and tasks at one time. This means there isn't enough capacity and many of those personal tasks drop off the list completely.

There are (at least) two things wrong with this.

Many women are exhausted and have lost a sense of self and personal identity, and often hate themselves for allowing it to happen (Just me?).

We've been told from every direction that we are not good looking enough, unlikeable, over-emotional, boring, or untalented. So, to fill that gap, we buy more products to improve our lives. (Thanks capitalist advertising!)

Except it's not just our fault. Society still allows it to happen.

I saw a meme recently that sums it up with something like…

*"Why do we make women buy beauty products to make themselves look less tired, but we don't do anything about actually helping women to BE less tired?"*

The other thing that this inequality around external priorities does, is actually dis-empower men, (and older children) from being self-sufficient, domestic, collaborative, and possibly even feeling a sense of importance and value. You could argue that women taking on more of these roles just allows laziness, but 'lazy' usually has an underlying cause. Perhaps it's an unintentional dis-engagement from these aspects of life because everything has already been taken care of, and it's hard to 'teach an old dog new tricks.' It isn't just laziness, it's also an element of conditioning, an absence of self-awareness, or lack of decision to provide proactive support. Just because as women we CAN do things efficiently and effectively, it doesn't mean we should naturally take on those jobs.

The goal is that we would ALL be able to choose what our priorities are, and not allow external pressures to squash them.

But it is difficult. It's not an easy overnight fix to re-organise your to-do list. I'm sure we'd all love to quit work and start getting daily massages and eating delicious healthy food for every meal. Taking up or returning to a hobby when we are caregiving to small children actually seems impossible. I get that. There have been lots of times when what I want to do as a priority just isn't possible, unless I took really small steps. Instead of trying to eat the whole damn elephant, we can just take one day at a time, and see what choice we could make in just one moment.

It might mean 5 mins of meditating instead of doom scrolling. Very hard. I know.

It might mean leaving a set of watercolour paints out on the desk to pop in and out of when there's a little minute.

It might mean saying no to volunteering at tuckshop and getting a massage or a coffee with a friend instead.

It's hard, with all that pressure we have on ourselves, but we can do more of what is good for us in a stealth way, and future you will thank you.

It is all just about considering what you're giving your energy to, if it's healthy, if it's working towards prioritising the things YOU want to prioritise, and if you can, start making small shuffles in that to-do list.

PART 1 - YOURSELF

# ACTIVITY - Mind Map Your Life

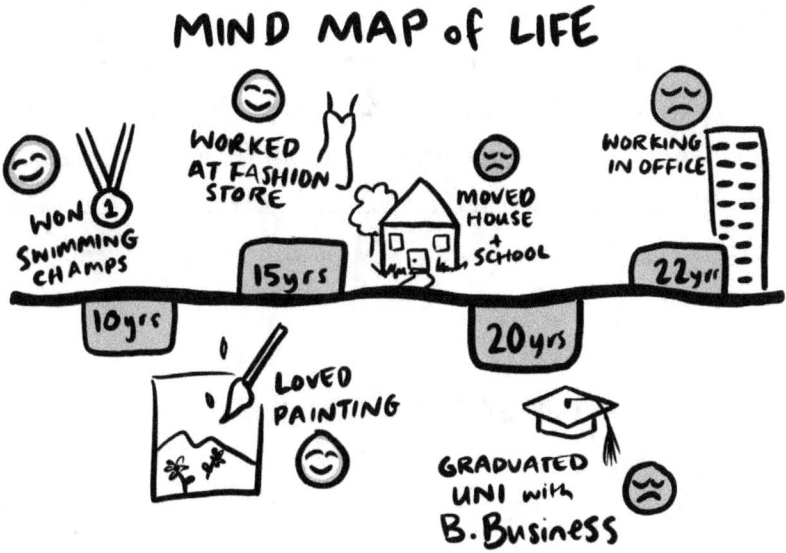

*Have you ever revisited your life achievements, milestones, defining moments? This is a great way to assess any patterns and common threads through life and work out what to keep and what to perhaps change.*

*Get a large piece of paper and pens and create a line from left to right as timeline of your life. The example is really rough, but you get the idea. Start on the left with childhood, think about*

- School and education
- Jobs
- Relationships
- Hobbies
- Dreams and goals

*Writing down any memories you feel comfortable to, make notes of*
*what happened*
*what you're proud of*
*what disappointments you had*
*use different colours to categorise, highlight key moments, and consider the recurring themes. I've used little smiles, and sad faces to say whether it was a happy or sad thing. This is a walk down memory lane to consider, be proud of, celebrate, analyse, identify how you felt about the events and activities of life, and work out what is next for you. What are the next steps towards your priorities?*

## MY MINDMAP OF LIFE

*Don't forget to download your workbook at www.making-lemonade.com.au/workbook. There's more space for these activities in there!*

# 6

## Recognising your PATTERNS

*"I'll be there in the corner thinking right over
Every single word of the conversation we just had
So, why am I like this?"*

—Orla Gartland

My brain is geared to collect data and organise it into patterns, to identify what's going on in the world. Which is not always cool, to be honest. Sometimes I'd rather just enjoy the moment being out with my friends instead of also observing how the couple across the bar are interacting with each other, noticing the common threads of fashion, or counting strangers' drink consumption. ADHD has been falsely labelled as an attention DEFICIT. When in fact, for me, it's an overload of data, paying too much attention, to everything that's going on in the room. It's having trouble regulating the over-attentiveness. It's hard to turn off but does wind down after a couple of margaritas.

Somewhere in my journey I turned this pattern observation on myself and started to notice some things. Recognising our repeating behaviours is the key to unlocking change in our lives. We can't redirect energy if we don't know where it's going in the first place. We can't shift our mood if we don't know what triggered it. We can't create more fruitful relationships if we don't notice how we interact with people.

What we can do is take a peek behind the curtain and see what's cooking inside our brains, and make a lifelong commitment to observe, critique and readjust.

## Identifying micro patterns of the self

It's not likely you'd be reading this book if there wasn't something you'd like to change. You're probably a person who is consistently observing and making adjustments to how you show up in the world. So, you might have actually identified something in your life you'd like to do better. This section is about how we can observe the cycles and patterns in our life, to better understand who we are and how we operate.

These patterns we develop aren't always easy to see and make change in, but it's definitely possible to do so.

I keep a close watch on the days of the month. This might be familiar if you're a person who menstruates. My hormonal cycle is highly impacting to my personality and emotions, which, as much as I try to 'control' this monthly diversion into what I can only describe as 'hell', it can be really difficult.

As a side note, the reason for this is a condition called PMDD. Pre-menstrual Dysphoric Disorder - where my hormones wreak havoc on my wellbeing and

I spend many days before my period with emotional irrationality, worsened depression, anxiety, anger, fatigue, bloating, and pain, also because of the endometriosis and adenomyosis. I'm not here to give the full medical explanations of my ailments, but just know that it's quite hellish, and I must continue to show up in life with it. If you're a person who menstruates, you may have your own challenges with this stuff. It's unfortunately quite common. I'm sorry.

After many years of dealing with the ups and downs of this condition, I have learned to observe the patterns, and make allowances and adjustments for the times when things get bad. I'll try not to schedule certain things around certain times of the month. I have explained the condition to my kids that it's like I'm Miss Hannagan, (from Annie the Musical) and will let them know when it's 'Miss Hannagan time!' while apologising.

It's being aware of my triggers, having plans in place and being kind to myself, so I don't ruin every relationship in my rampage of hormonal rage.

I guess one of the benefits of being born with male sex organs is having a generally stable and consistent hormone profile. However, this doesn't preclude you from having emotional patterns.

We all have things that set off emotional responses, sometimes they're random, often they're the same thing.

I had a big student loan debt back home in New Zealand. When I finished university it was $24k, over a few years I paid off $17k, but in 2015 it was around $32k. To me, this was completely unfair, I had taken a lot of time off work to raise babies, I had paid off such a big chunk, and I was in a worse off position than when I'd started. It INFURIATED me. I could not deal with any piece of correspondence about it. I would fly off the handle. I felt so trapped, disempowered, frustrated, betrayed by the NZ government... there were so many feelings. Initially this would just happen, I wouldn't realise it was happening. I'd get a letter from the government department, and the pot would start to boil, building into what was quite a destructive mood. I started to observe the pattern, (OK, and my husband at the time may have pointed it out) and started to try and deal with it in a certain way. Only when I mentally prepared myself and was aware of the potential response could I dampen it down to be able to be a grown-up about this shitty financial situation. Eventually I decided I wouldn't be paying another cent of it and went through a process to declare myself bankrupt in New Zealand. That fixed that!

And now I've given two examples of rage responses as micro patterns, but there are many other types. I do respond to things in ways other than anger, FYI.

We have many micro patterns in our:

- Thoughts
- Emotional responses
- Physical being
- Communication style
- Habits and routine

Observing these patterns is where you'll find the power to change. If this is something you haven't done before, give yourself some time. Take a couple of months to start noticing things that come in cycles. Becoming more aware, finding acceptance, and building a life around the 'knowing' of what makes us unique will lead to a more resilient and happy existence.

PART 1 - YOURSELF

The key to changing any of these things is to first assess them. Because you need to understand WHY things are the way they are. Understanding WHY creates space between you and the pattern, it suggests you could observe before you act. The best shifts I've made in my life are the ones where I have investigated the reasons behind a pattern, found self-compassion, and then taken action. I feel better about it, I'm not treating my behaviours as a crime to be punished, I'm approaching it with gentleness and encouragement.

So, as you investigate these patterns over time, take it easy on yourself. Most of the 'negative' things you find are probably coping mechanisms for some other reason. You don't have to change everything at once, and it doesn't have to be every day, just tackle one at a time. Start with the obvious things that really bother you.

our brains are strange

## THOUGHT PATTERNS
**How do you speak to yourself?**

This is BIG and can be HARD. Neural pathways carve their way through our brains like a river, and it can be very hard to redirect a river, unless you're a beaver.

What does the internal monologue say when you've messed up? What about when you've achieved something? What are those carved out stories you automatically tell yourself all day long?

For example, I can be a pretty chronic negative thinker. Due to lifelong patterns, I generally feel undeserving and 'not good enough.' This impacts my stress levels, how I approach life tasks, and how I interact with people. It's well carved in and takes some really conscious effort to recognise and look at it objectively. It can be so difficult to undo years of internal dialogue that has been throwing shit at you all day every day. I don't even want to repeat the things I say to myself at times, I would NEVER talk to another human as terribly as I do to myself.

In addition, I feel like my neuro-spicy brain is constantly looking for problems, because solving problems gives me dopamine (a chemical that is found to be quite deficient in those with ADHD). However, there are so many problems in this world, that sometimes that's all I see.

But it's possible to shift it, just in small steps.

So, I aim to carve new pathways. I do this by looking for good, positive, uplifting, beautiful things. Noticing and appreciating little nice things.

Because I think life is made up of BIG CHALLENGES and small joys.

I'll be walking along, and literally force myself to think a thought about something nice, like "Look at that fucking sunshine today, that's amazing... ISN'T IT JADE?!"

If you are finding yourself trash talking in your brain, observe it gently, don't get stuck beating yourself up for beating yourself up, and work towards quietening that voice.

Proactively talking positively to ourselves sounds like a cliche, but it does really work. Retraining your mind to spot the good things in life with some gratitude, or congratulating yourself when you've achieved something big or small, makes a difference to our wellbeing.

## EMOTIONAL RESPONSES
**What are your triggers?**

I have panic attacks. (Gosh I'm not painting a great picture of my emotional life in this book, am I?)

I've had them since I was a teenager. I'm so masterful at them, I've actually learnt how to have one without anyone even knowing. There are a few triggers, sometimes it's social anxiety in a new situation where I don't feel like I have a 'safe' person, or if there are several issues I'm juggling all at the same time, or a big one is if I feel like, or I actually messed something up. I hate, hate, hate to think that someone would think I'm incompetent or sloppy, that I didn't do a good enough job at something. So please think about people's mental health before you go sending that trolling email!

Sometimes, it comes on for no reason at all, my whole body turns hot and prickly, my heart starts a palpitation party and I feel like the world is about to end. Some of the emotions that come with these triggers are crying, anger, frustration, and sadness.

When I started addressing the small version of Jade who learned coping strategies because she felt unsafe sometimes, I diminished the impact. With the help of psychological professionals, I learned that instead of compounding my anxiety, with anxiety about the anxiety, I could separate myself from it, turn to it, and find out what it was all about.

It's literally talking to myself "Ah. OK. You're anxious. That makes sense because of XY and Z, but we are safe - we're just grocery shopping." (I mean, that induces panic in any regular person doesn't it?!) Or I tell myself, "You're all good. We're hanging out with people who love us." Maybe I might need to remove myself to regulate again, so I treat myself kindly and do just that.

Not every emotional response will be a panic attack or a fit of rage, as I have demonstrated. It's super important to observe what triggers other types of emotions, like how joy comes when you achieve something, or you get inspired when you help somebody else, or you feel melancholic through the winter months. The more you know about your emotional landscape, the better!

# COMMUNICATION STYLE

**Have you ever considered the way you communicate?**

I know as a neurodivergent person; this topic comes up a lot as a key aspect. The cliche is that autistic people are blunt and direct, don't like small talk, don't make eye contact, and lack empathy. Well, for me, apart from the small talk thing, much of this is the opposite, which might be why I've flown under the radar for so long. I want to be more direct and confident in my communication, but am very considered, anxious and a bit people-pleasing in what I say and feel so deeply in empathy that it's almost a suffering. Probably to my detriment, I am personally quite over-conscious about how I communicate, but I know this isn't the case for many people.

Taking stock of the way you communicate, and the way you'd like to be communicated with can have some really positive impacts on relationships and social interaction. Some things to consider might be:

Do people engage with you comfortably?
Are you considering the other person's responses?
How do you feel about small talk?
Do you notice that you often wish you'd said something, but didn't?
Do people stare at you blankly when you're talking?
What is your body doing when you're talking with certain people?
Can you tell when someone is disinterested?
How do you give and receive feedback?
Maybe you are really direct and find yourself putting people offside sometimes.
Are you a good listener?
Maybe you love chit chat and small talk and shooting the breeze.
Do you find yourself in arguments often?
Maybe you only talk when it's really necessary.
Maybe you prefer email to phone calls.

Thinking about this can open up new ways to relate to people, with different opportunities for connection and showing up in the world.

**Mindful communication?** Do you take a moment before engaging with people, to think about what you're saying and what the intentions are? As an anxious neurodivergent person, I probably spend too much time considering these things. But I'm not always in this zone.

It's easy not to give our communication a second thought. After all, we've been talking since we were toddlers, it's a natural, automated process.

But what if we were just a bit more mindful, slowed down, became curious, truly listened and connected with people instead of rushing in with our agendas and preconceived ideas.

You don't have to start walking around like a Zen guru, but I've found that thinking about communication like this can bring a calmness to situations and makes the most of conversations.

# PHYSICAL

### What's your physical context like?

Do you have some patterns in your physical being that impact your sense of wellbeing? If you sit at your desk too long, does your lower back get sore? What physical ailments do you have, and do you know their triggers?

If you're a menstruating person, it's good to track that cycle, and see what it does in your physical and emotional body.

Whenever you visit a doctor about an illness or something bothering you, they will ask for info about the patterns. So, it can help to keep a diary to track stuff.

Another physical aspect to consider in your pattern tracking, is your surroundings.

So, another honest story from me, I am quite messy. I also really crave order and minimalism, but I'm like Jekyll and Hyde in a lot of things.

This used to annoy me about myself, and I'd get really frustrated. I still do, but I'm more compassionate towards myself about it, because I noticed what happens and why. If I'm really busy, sick, hyperfocused on a project, stuff just collects in little parties around my home. Also, I have children, and need to keep reminding myself that I cannot have order while they live here. Additionally, my ADHD causes me to leave things out where I can see them, because I'm scared I'm going to forget about them. This is what's known as 'doom piles.' They're everywhere around my apartment, but to make me feel better, I've taken to putting them in baskets. However, sometimes the doom piles get so big, that whatever I left out deliberately to remember, ends up on the bottom and gets forgotten about. All that aside to say, if your physical context affects you, what are the patterns? Are you mad when there is lots of laundry sitting around. Are you happy and more productive when the kitchen bench is clean? Looking at patterns in our body and our environment can really identify areas to work on, or things to keep doing.

## HABITS and ROUTINE

**This is a big one, people write entire books about it.**

An assessment of the habits and routine we keep is a really good place to start with any changes we might want to make. These are the building blocks that make up the hours and days of our lives. (Like sands through the hourglass...)

Here's a bit of a different take - let's say routine is the allocation of task to time, and habits are how we go about those tasks.

My routine might be doing laundry on a Sunday morning, but my habit is that I don't hang things properly on the clothesline.

So routine is like a deliberate action, and habits are the more unconscious method in which we undertake the action.

Regardless of the definition, I know I sometimes just feel a bit shit about the hum drum of daily life. So, I need to look at my routine and habits. Is it because I haven't had enough walking in my routine, and I've gotten in the habit of sleeping in until 7 a.m.? Probs. I love sleeping in, so it took a few months to build some exercise back into my routine. I use an app to track my steps, and this helps me know how I'm going.

Talking about habits, I have already shared about my relationship to drinking and the problems it has caused. So, my routine was to do some kind of relaxation, but my habit was to use alcohol to do so. I've somehow managed to get a hold of this relationship many times through the years, as my reliance on alcohol has come and gone.

After my separation, it ramped up. I'm deliberately trying not to apply negative language to this, because you may be struggling in this area, and wherever you're at, the last thing you need is judgment. But I wasn't in a good place. If we put it this way, I was consuming much more than the health department would recommend. Excusing it because of what I'd been through, and that I was 'just having fun' in my newly single life.

I don't know that binge watching streaming TV and binge drinking wine all alone is the healthiest way to have fun.

Now, there's a cultural norm where wine and mums go hand-in-hand, so I just felt like it was a normal thing to be doing. You might even be thinking that, and you'd be right. We have this weird thing where we accept alcohol abuse as normal in our culture, but geez, if you smoke pot, wow, what a loser. I digress into cultural context, which we'll get into more in part three.

So, I was obviously extremely depressed, and one night after being out drinking, got home to an empty house and lost my mind. I won't go into detail, but waking up the next day, to some serious messages and missed calls from friends was a real wakeup call that I had to change something. But first, I had to examine WHY I was doing it.

I was trying to suppress my loneliness, fill a void, and escape from the pain of feeling like a failure. I was also quite sick at the time with my Chiari Malformation issues, so there were multiple reasons why I had developed this coping mechanism.

Talking through this with my psychologist helped me understand those hard feelings are normal, given the circumstances. And my homework was to try and just be with them instead of escaping through changing my mental state. Turn to the hard feelings, offer compassion, be prepared to be uncomfortable, and understand that there is a big journey to processing the hurt that comes with the end of a marriage.

Now, I didn't quit alcohol cold turkey, I can't tell you that I'm 5 years sober, that is not how I did it. I just chose to shift a habit and change the importance drinking had in my life. I prioritised healing and personal work, canceled the wine subscription, switched to a soda based drink, and didn't have any booze in the house through the week.

I forced myself into exercising more, and slowly started to feel improvement. Yes, sometimes I still drink, but not in a mindless, needy kind of way. For me it was about having compassion towards my inner self for developing a coping strategy habit, and gently working towards being present with life, instead of the opposite.

I want to acknowledge that this approach may not work for all people. Addiction is real, and you may require professional help with it. I certainly do NOT want to tell you to 'try mindfulness.' It's never as simple as that. But taking stock of habits, good and bad, help you understand more about who you are and where you're at. There might be things you want to change, or new habits you'd rather implement.

# ACTIVITY - Get Unstuck

*Sometimes there might be something we want to change, but it just seems too hard. Some things are. There can be circumstances that prohibit a shift in priority or pattern, or we get a bit stuck trying to work out how we can move.*

*Use this model to journal through feelings of 'stuckness' and see if you can determine a way forward, OR just come to peace with what is... for now. Everything changes eventually.*

## THE SITUATION

*Write down everything you can about the challenge you're facing. All the positives and negatives, what's irking you, what you're dealing with well, what it actually is.*

## THE OPTIONS

*Now brainstorm what the options are. What alternatives are there to the situation. You could rank them from viable to ridiculous.*

## THE DECISION

*What tends to happen then, is that something will come bubbling to the surface as the most viable, logical, or highly desired option.*

## THE PLAN

*Now that you have an idea of the way forward, create a plan. Set a time-based goal. Write out the steps you need to take to get into the space you're looking towards. Make the plan.*

*You can do this for as many stuck situations as you like. Whether it's being stuck in a job you dislike, a relationship that should be over, or you're stuck NOT doing something you want to incorporate into life - like making art or learning music... see how this framework works for you.*

*For more scribbling space, download your free workbook at www.making-lemonade.au/workbook*

# 7

## *Checking your Mental Health*

*"Where's your head at?"*

—Basement Jaxx

It's all well and good to talk about defining preferences, setting priorities, and recognising patterns, but there can be some really challenging obstacles when we struggle with our mental health.

I've had so many diagnoses for the way my brain works, I have quite an understanding of many different conditions. It first started with a depression diagnosis at 17 at a university medical clinic. But I was self-medicating for paralysing anxiety at night time and dealing with severe mood issues at the age of 12. I've collected a few magic beans through the years when I've sought out help.

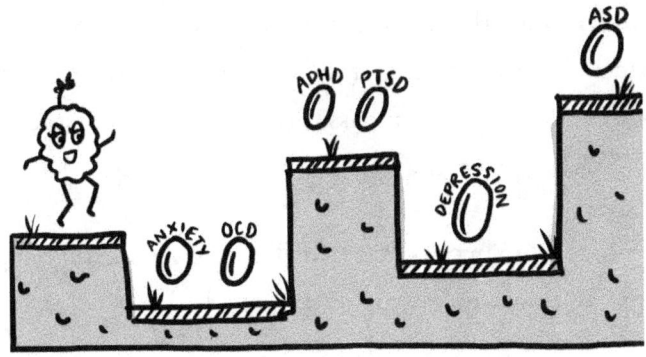

In addition to this, in the last couple of years I have been diagnosed autistic. What!? It came as quite the surprise. This doesn't discount the symptoms and pathology of these previously diagnosed conditions, but more, explains it.

On the one hand, I could say that this, for me, has been a hindrance to fully understanding myself. On the other hand, I have spent so many hours exploring these conditions, attending therapy with a special interest in the idea of self and psychology, it makes perfect sense.

If you're like me, you might get a bit mad about being 'a bit mad.' I get so frustrated at my mental health, and that is really unhelpful. I've heard someone say that anxiety is worrying about things that haven't happened, and PTSD is worry about things that have already happened happening again. Feels so true to me. However, it could actually be said that those who navigate mental health challenges are the strongest in mind. We must become self-aware about the activity of our psyche and it's corresponding behavior, the impact that has on our health and wellbeing, and how it affects our relationship with others. This makes for some real resilience building!

But we haven't all come to that place within ourselves.

I sometimes find myself so focused on my mental conditions that I become a bit self-centered. I forget that the best way out of a funk is to help someone else. I forget to move away from being afraid and anxious and go into situations that make me feel that way with compassion and curiosity. I just forget about the good stuff. That's what mental disease does. It's dis - ease.

We can get very caught up in ourselves in different ways, having a big impact on relationships and how we show up in the world.

We harbor fears of being left out, so can be defensive.
We hide from the world in a pit of low self-worth.
We cast judgments on others to diminish own shortcomings.
We avoid conflict so we fail to put boundaries in place.
We run towards conflict and inflict harm on ourselves and our relationships.
Sometimes we want to be right, more than we want to be loving.

Challenges with mental health can create all these scenarios within ourselves, which is why it's so important to get that objective self-perspective.

Trauma can make you hyper-vigilant because at some point you were under threat or experienced danger. Your nervous system attunes to potential risks and activates your best protective mechanisms, which can be different for everyone. Some of mine are people pleasing, staying small, being overly adaptable, and almost constant anxiety. But at least I am somewhat aware that I'm doing these things, and I can work on solutions. What are you robbing the world of by succumbing to these self-protective measures?

No one is better than you.
No one is less than you.
We are all in this together.

When you go with care, love, connection, and curiosity it gives you purpose and confidence despite the maladaptive ways we've developed.

Personally, I started enjoying things more by being kinder to myself, and realising every moment was an opportunity for learning or joy. Obviously now, I go about my day with a trail of bluebirds and butterflies as I embrace every chance to experience the wonders of life in a perpetual state of MINDFULNESS.

LOL.

No. I do not. Sometimes I sob myself to sleep, washing off all my eye creams, because I feel like a failure at life. And it'll probably be just because I picked up on a micro-emotion of a colleague which made me think they don't like me.

I might beat myself up in the bathroom mirror because I didn't say what I should have said to protect my personal values.

I hold myself back big time because I'm so afraid of rejection.

Common advice is to try and change these things about ourselves. I get that. Life would be a bit easier if we could. But what may be an unpopular opinion in positive psychology is that sometimes we can't eradicate the negative, and it's right there, front and centre.

Sometimes, the neural pathways of depression are so lit up that I cannot fathom enjoying ice cream.

Sometimes the most mindful I can be is acknowledging that I hate the world.

Sometimes I just get lost in all the problems I have.

So, I think we just have to work with the quirk.

How?

Well... here are a few thoughts...

For me, fighting against what my brain is doing creates more chaos. Accepting that I will have these down times, angry times, and negative thoughts allows a channel of self-love to open up inside me. I try to look at my perceived flaws as part of who I am, accept that a previous version of myself was just trying to survive, and work out ways to move through WITH it.

I'm a people pleaser? That means I can offer really great service in my business. But I also need to set boundaries.

Social anxiety is giving me grief? I'm going to pretend it's excitement, then deliberately work myself into a social situation that might be challenging and discover that I don't die. Even if I say something stupid.

Chronic overthinker? Time to get my thoughts out on paper and write some musings, it's how this book was born!

Instead of trying to run from these characteristics, I'd like to work out ways to turn towards them and find something productive I can do with them. I don't want them to leak into relationships or take over my life, but I also can't just shove them down and pretend that they don't exist.

Taking care of my mental health is letting me be me, embracing all my flaws and allowing myself to work with the quirk! What does it mean for you to take care of your mental health? Do you turn from the hard feelings, or ask yourself what you need when they come up?

PART 1 - YOURSELF

# ACTIVITY - What helps my mental health?

*Circle the tricks that you know help your mental health stay on track. Fill in the blanks for any others that aren't mentioned here. You can refer to this page when you need a reminder of what's essential for your journey.*

# MY MENTAL HEALTH HELPERS

# 8

## *Taking Personal Responsibility*

*"Welcome to your life, there's no turning back."*

—Tears for Fears

I have to say though, having mental health challenges is not a free pass to be an asshole. It might mean we mess up, and we can hope that those we spend our time with (or cancel on) will have empathy and understanding. But it's not an excuse to be consistently shitty to other people.

What does being a bit 'shitty' look like?

- Cancelling or rearranging plans frequently.
- Allowing difficult emotions to overflow into relationships and not repairing.
- Never apologizing.
- Mistaking hurtful comments for 'honesty.'
- Expecting people to do things the way YOU want to do them, too often.
- Not owning mistakes.
- Being judgmental about other people's shitty behaviour.

I know, because I'm sure I've been this person at times, and will likely be at times, even if I don't mean it. The key is that awareness of self, and communicating well. I overcommit at times, and as much as I want to make plans happen, sometimes I just can't and it's probably annoying for my friends. But I will try to make effort to communicate about why.

Our interpersonal connections are a great source of anxiety, friction, worry, anger, frustration, but also our greatest source of joy, contentment, purpose, love, and life itself.

Relationships are about give and take, and some people's tolerance for 'take' might be quite high. I'd say mine is quite high, but there have been times where I've just had enough. And there have been times where people have had enough of me, too.

Friendships come and go, some last a long time, some just a short season. It's a part of the ebb and flow and growth in life.

But I want to talk about personal responsibility. It's something that could be a bit touchy, but I notice this everywhere I go. In work, in friendships, in relationships, in restaurants, on the road - it's that people love to deflect. We love to deflect blame and responsibility for things going wrong. There's always another reason why, someone else to blame, or we are the victim of something. Sometimes, this is true, but often, we jump to defensiveness way too quickly, without examining our own part to play in a situation.

It's simply a protection mechanism. Coming back to that idea that people often want to make themselves seem better than they think they are, we don't want to look like we've done wrong.

PART 1 - YOURSELF

Kids do this alllll the time.

Let's take a kid example:

Me: OK kid, what happened?

Them, pointing at the other one: THEY did XYZ and that made ME do XYZ.

That's the response of an underdeveloped brain, but I see adults doing this too. People get stuck there, on the wrongs that others have done to them.

What if we released all that we are trying to control and became more curious, more compassionate and more connected? What if we examined what our responsibility is? To manage our emotions. To take the right action. To repair relationships. To know our boundaries. To choose how we let things affect us.

I have to frequently remind myself:

YOU ARE NOT IMMUNE TO THE TROUBLES OF LIFE.

Let's get out of the mindset of "why did this happen to me?"

It's happened because we exist in a world where we come up against lots of variables in our path to 'success.' You're special, but not THAT special - I'm pretty sure best selling blogger and author Mark Manson says something similar. Hard times will come, we will feel big feelings, but if we understand our own modus operandi, and approach the challenges with bravery and self-acceptance, we can get through anything.

I get it. I understand. I get stuck on the 'wrongs' too. But over time, I've learned that working towards owning my own life means those wrongs have less power over me.

Don't be a victim. Easy to say, but not as easy to do. Easy to think you're not. But what lies underneath our psyche that we haven't yet addressed?

There are things that happen in everyone's life that we latch onto as a defining moment. There are TERRIBLE things that happen to us. Damaging, traumatising, or unfair things. But once it's a defining moment, you can decide on the definition.

You can change the definition of your defining moments.

You might wallow, play victim, be depressed, sad, angry. That's all normal, but allow time to shift your perspective. Allow time to heal you and find the lessons in challenges. There is always darkness, but you couldn't have light without darkness, they need each other to exist. You can find the light. It might be the tiniest pinprick of light. It's always there. It might just be the nurse helping you at your mother's deathbed, or a compliment you received yesterday, or your child's smile, but there is always a way to take ownership of the scenario and discover the light.

Once you learn to see both dark and light, you can see that there are lessons to be learned in our mistakes.

So, if you make a mistake, just own it.

In firmer words, Own. Your. Shit.

How? What does that MEAN?

If you know yourself better, you can do this better. This will give you the platform of confidence to take the responsibility to repair whatever cracks your behaviour might have caused. It's OK to mess up. It's normal to make mistakes. (I am preaching to myself here.) It is totally natural to be imperfect. But if you fuck up, and you own it, it's really hard for someone else to be mad at you, therefore you can reduce conflict in your life.

Sometimes we deflect to try and make ourselves seem better than we think we are, in order to avoid any conflict. But deflecting and trying to hide the errors makes people much madder, because it's dishonest. So, we end up with internal AND external conflict, rather than just diffusing a situation by being open, honest, vulnerable and owning your own stuff. I will say this again, because it's important:

It's very hard for someone to be mad at you when you honestly own your own shit.

If you are someone who finds it hard to apologise, examine this in yourself. Explore why that is. Maybe it's got a lot to do with shame.

I am no expert in shame, but if you need one, seek out the work of Brené Brown. I'm an expert in my own shame, of which I have dealt with quite a lot. It can get quite complicated, and I don't fully understand how we hold on to shame, especially around events or behaviours that happen TO us, and that we did nothing to instigate - e.g., abuse. But I think shame is tangled in our reluctance to take personal responsibility.

When we experience this trauma, humiliation or rejection, feelings of shame build. As a kid, if we don't have the right tools, support, or love to counter-act the shame, we start to develop coping mechanisms to deal with our own flailing sense of self-worth.

So, let's talk about taking responsibility despite shame.

I've done some stupid things in my time. I'm sure you have too. But they're only stupid in hindsight. If we know it's stupid at the time we probably wouldn't do it, right?

What usually happens with the realization of our own 'stupidity,' is shame. And shame is crippling. What can we do?

I believe what feeds shame is the avoidance of owning problems and mistakes. We try to control other people's perception of us by distancing ourselves from the problem. Ugh, this doesn't work. But there is something you can do about this shame. This is what I try (and often fail but keep trying) to do. Take responsibility for your actions. Own them. Do what you need to make it right, and then you can say you've done your best with that situation.

**You learn faster by owning your mistakes.**
**You own your mistakes by believing you are worthy to move on.**

If you own your mistakes, you might still feel shame, but it eliminates the ability of anyone else to criticise you. Here's an example.

A number of years ago when I was applying for a higher role in my job, I stumbled across the interview questions on the printer at work.

I read them.

Then I went back to my desk and made notes about what I could remember.

Then I felt bad, and I pondered what the right thing to do was. Honesty and integrity are super important to me, and I felt like what I'd just done was not aligned to those values.

So, I figured I had a couple of choices. I could have just let myself have the advantage and prepare for the interview according to what intel I'd just gathered. Or I could screw up the paper and throw it in the bin. Another choice, that I came up with, was that I could tell my manager, who was the panel chair, that I'd seen the questions.

In my mind, that was the action I could take that represented the highest amount of ownership, and the least amount of shame.

So, I did two things. I screwed up the paper and put it in the bin, and I went to my boss and told her that I'd seen the questions on the printer. She asked me if I read them, and I told her 'yes'.

She said, "Thanks for being so honest." And I left that scenario with integrity, fully owning what I'd done. I also nailed the new interview questions and got the job.

It was scary to tell someone I admired and who supported me that I'd fucked up, but it felt so good. Nobody could criticise my integrity in that situation, I'd done everything I could.

Sometimes when you try to right the wrongs, the other party might not be so cool about it, and that's the risk you run. There's no control over that, all you can do is take the action that aligns with your own values, know that you've done YOUR best, and leave the rest of it to the gods.

# PART 2 - OTHERS

# 9

## Part 2 Introduction - Connecting with Others

*"He ain't heavy, he's my brother."*

—The Hollies

There are actually few things more important than the people in our immediate sphere. These are the humans we have an impact on. Like, really, is there anything more important? We. We are in this crazy ride together. The humans we are connected to are the whole point of this circus.

In my own life, I've seen so much care and amazing connection with people. But it's taken some time to get to, I've struggled with relationships for a number of reasons, being undiagnosed autistic for most of my life has been a really big part of that. But I have always believed that connection and relationship is the solution to all that ails humanity. The trouble is it can be a bumpy ride to understanding. Traveling alone is only good when it's to Southeast Asia on your 23rd birthday. Perfect adventure. But a life journey must be shared. With whoever is in our midst.

There are lots of 'self-help' books on becoming a better communicator. Plenty of tips and tricks about listening, and leadership, and all that. You know there'll be some flavour of that here. But it's all pointless, if you don't know WHY you are trying to improve.

It must be for beings, not things. Your family. Your friends. Your colleagues. Your dog! Not for houses, or belongings, or projects. They are empty shells without the humans and creatures behind them.

This doesn't mean that we must create deep connections with every single person, but there can be love, even in brief interactions.

We have people in our lives that are super short-term engagements.

Then there are others who have a bit more time.

Then there are some we could spend a weekend with.

And then there's those who are life partners, unlimited friendships, could talk forever. Not everyone can have all the love and all the time, we might be able to think about it in this way:

**Jade's TIME/LOVE Model:**

Just to clarify, 'love' covers all kinds of respect, affection and like that we feel for people. So, Nearest and Dearest – that's our close family, best friends, lovers and partners. The 'Wish we could' group are those amazing people we love, but hardly get any time with. We probably want to start a commune with them. The Friendly Strangers are our work colleagues, the lovely barista we get our morning coffee from, maybe mums from school. And the Background Extras, well, you'll know who they are. High school mates, old friends who've become acquaintances, people like that. Probably friends on Facebook but wouldn't actually talk in real life.

So when I'm talking about connecting with people, mostly I'm talking about the first 3 quarters of the quadrant. The Background Extras aren't really a group to be focused on. The others all are.

We land in this world without a say in who we're attached to. (Or unattached to.) One thing is for sure is that relationships and break ups and break downs are significant lemons in life.

We just get born to a couple of randos and have no say in what happens to us from then on. From day one we are building a foundation of how to relate, relying solely on those random people, whether present or not, to give us everything we need. As I'm sure you are aware, lots of people do not know how to give tiny humans what they need. Parents in the 80s were NOT reading blogs about attachment theory, and if you were an accidental surprise, then life probably became very difficult for them. Your needs were probably neglected a little bit, depending on a few factors.

Or you might have been lucky enough to win the birth lotto into a loving, safe, attached environment, and you're perfectly stable. You probably don't need this book then, put it away.

But it's not just the significant relationships, we interact with thousands of people in our lifetime, and even a chance encounter can impact your life in a massive way.

We have all kinds of groups of people in our lives, some closer than others, and some with more meaningful relationships than others. But by doing even a small amount of work in all our interpersonal interactions, we can probably have a more fulfilled life.

I will talk about my own (sometimes awkward) ways of relating to people and share some things I've learned along the way. We continue this never-ending journey of self-improvement. Why? For yourself, yes, but also the people around you. Life is much more fun when you get on well with people, they are arguably our greatest source of joy. A margarita at the beach is joyful, but much more so laughing about life with a dear friend, right?

So, seeing as our lives are all interconnected, and we deal with people all the time, it's actually one of the most important things you could do, is to learn a bit more about how to communicate and connect effectively, and have healthy relationships.

What if we released all that we are trying to control and became more curious, more compassionate and more connected.

Anxiety is soaring at rapid rates, and this usually means we are often operating out of a need for survival. When we're in survival mode, we display the following types of characteristics:

Protective
Defensive
Impatient
Selfish
Suspicious
Competitive
Controlling
Anger
Frustration
Over thinking
Busy
Inconsiderate
Hurrying

We have a narrow view of the world and underlying feeling that there is lack and limited resources.

When we develop alternate ways of operating, learn how to soothe that protective survival instinct, and seek to be better in ourselves, and better for others, we are thriving. When we are in this space we are:

Compassionate
Connected
Content
Welcoming

Generous
Calm
Kind
Considerate
Friendly
Humorous
Aware
Open

I know which space I'd rather be in. It makes for a much nicer experience interacting with other humans if I can get myself into a space that feels safer.

Of course, there is going to be conflict, awkwardness, discomfort, and all kinds of emotions when it comes to relating to people, regardless of which state we're in. There's no avoiding the hard stuff, we must be prepared for that. But I believe and have seen in my own life, that we can minimise it and move through it with relationships intact. Not every conflict has to mean the end of connection, and we can find ways to be more connected in our day to day lives.

# 10

## Feeling Disconnected

*"But I've been burned and I've been down so many times*
*We walk in circles, the blind leading the blind*
*We've been disconnected somehow"*

—Keane

We are in a time in history of major transition. Maybe we always are, but in my lifetime I've gone from having a three-digit phone number on a turn dial telephone in rural New Zealand, to having several powerful personal computer devices at my disposal. This rapid change in our lives is a common discussion, but sometimes I think people talk about it like we chose this magnetism to the small black rectangles in our hands.

We didn't really choose it, it kind of just happened to us. Technology for personal devices had a life of its own and wormed its way in to our lives. It has created a dependency. It has opened worlds of possibility, and our brains are just trying to keep up.

As we passively go about our lives, we have allowed the change to happen to us, and it's very hard to step out of it. We're like frogs in a slow boiling pot.

As new values have emerged, old ones have gone by the wayside. I think phones, although supposedly keeping us connected, are playing a significant role in human disconnection, and it's mostly subconscious. We inadvertently now view this black rectangle as the number one resource for connection, activity, and opportunity, and if it's not going on here, then is it really living?

Here's a thought. I think the addictive activity going on in our brains with phone use, makes us more anxious. We are kind of like skittish junkies wandering around nervous and confused. Because our brains are addicted to phones, we spend more time in limbic system mode of fight or flight. AKA survival mode.

This frightened disconnection is everywhere. I feel it in myself. When anxiety is high, everything and everyone feels like a threat.

The other significant aspect of disconnection I believe is trauma. There are real, and serious reasons why someone's nervous system ends up in a traumatised state. With more and more discussion about the impact of trauma on humans, and I'd go as far to say, that most people around us carry the hurts of traumatic experiences, and we should treat each other gently because of this. I think we could safely say that at a minimum, the events of 2020 have left some distinctive marks on our mental health, and even years later some people are still feeling the effects.

Trauma is not necessarily the event, but it is the person's response to the event.

Two people could experience the same type of event, but one person has extreme PTSD and the other perhaps anxiety, but it doesn't affect them as much. Judging someone's trauma based on what the event was, is nobody's job. Everyone has a different story as to what brought them to that place.

So what might be worth considering is looking at your own perception of what trauma is, for yourself, and for others. It's OK to discover many years later, that something that happened to you, was in fact very traumatic. If you do, I highly recommend talking to a professional about it. This was my own personal experience. For many years I thought that things that happened to me were a) my own fault and b) totally normal. But I came to some realisations later in life that they were not normal, OK, or something I should have to live with. With help from amazing therapists, I've been able to get clarity on things that were lingering and move forward with acceptance. (And great meds.)

**Does everyone have at least a low-grade, unconscious anxiety about being 'excommunicated from the group,' which is made worse by addiction to technology?**

Now I do not proclaim to be any kind of neuroscientist, this is just all stuff I've picked up along the way, so don't take it as gospel.

Though I am particularly interested in psychology, and communication and as per a lot of discussion on the internet, there is a pretty common narrative about our brains in this modern age. We might know about the fight or flight response, and the reptilian brain that keeps us on high alert. Our nervous system is geared to perceive threats and respond accordingly.

In days long ago, the threats were things like war, famine, beasts and vampires, pterodactyls, and the wrath of God.

For the average person living a privileged life in the western world, there aren't actually that many physical threats in our day-to-day. As we cruise through this cushy modern life, most situations are pretty safe. Yet, we seem to be more anxious than ever. Our systems are on high alert and responding accordingly. The give-away signs are things like

Avoiding eye contact
Emotional sensitivity
Decreased empathy
Irritability

You only have to leave your house once a day to see people demonstrating these kinds of things.

These are the characteristics of a ramped up nervous system response.

These are the characteristics of disconnection.

Communication skills seem to have deteriorated as we hide behind our devices. We have forgotten the lost art of manners and casual chit chat. Is this just normal city life? Am I in a bubble? Do I think other people are like this because I am?

Is it the 24 hour news cycle, highlighting to us all the potential things that COULD happen?

Or is it that we are so busy and addicted to our phones that we struggle to distinguish things that are perfectly safe? Like, people around us.

Is addiction to our phones some kind of FOMO?! (Fear of Missing Out)

Let's talk about this FOMO for a minute.

As we talked about in part 1, we're social creatures, we feel safer when we are part of the group. Many animals are like this, and whether you believe we are animals or something else, there seems to be common understanding that this is how we roll. Humans want to be part of the group. We need each other. We need our family of origin. We need friendships. We need to feel accepted, loved, welcomed, and connected, to live our best lives.

So, when I talk about FOMO, it's really about loneliness.

Perhaps it's this innate protection system that understands if we are alone, we are vulnerable, if we are with group, we are safe. I personally have a general uneasiness no matter what I'm doing. This is the beauty of PTSD, anxiety, or whatever other bloody mental condition is cropping up for me on any given day.

What I wonder though, is this:
If we FEEL alone, do we feel unsafe, and our system activates?
Or is it just if we are physically alone?

I feel like it's the first one. We feel alone, and it heightens our nervous system. When we spend all that time looking at other people through our phone screens, maybe that activates FOMO, and therefore, loneliness.

Maybe our nervous systems haven't caught up to the fact that we're actually mostly safe from physical threat in this modern world. Maybe our nervous systems are really fucking scrambled, and we're subconsciously expecting the others to help and tend to us, because we actually feel like a threatened and injured member of the herd. Instead of everyone reaching out to tend to each other and keep each other safe, we're fretting for our own safety. In some ways we are all injured, and we all need tending to, so shouldn't we all be creating a practice in our lives that contributes to the wellbeing and assistance of others?

I think we can feel lonely in a crowd, and we can feel connected when we're alone.

Feelings of loneliness are wreaking havoc on humans all over the place, despite there being more people on earth than ever before. So, it must be the perception (or reality for some) of being alone, being away from the group, that disconnects us from each other and activates this system. Staring at our devices watching other people doing fun stuff probably doesn't help this.

What I'm getting at, is that whatever the science, the reality is that we feel safer, calmer, more in control, if we feel we are part of something. And the opposite if we're not.

PART 2 - OTHERS

Over recent history, there have been improvements in quality of life for a lot of people on earth, and we get to live longer. Hooray!...? We might have worked out how to tend to some of the body health challenges, but mental health challenges are on the rise.

Sometimes, no matter how much I tell myself I'm safe and doing OK, that anxious fretting just doesn't leave. It wants to stop me from doing things because everything seems unsafe.

These high alert brains continue to activate an anxious system that serves to protect our resources, social standing, and energy. When we're experiencing a difficult situation, our brain makes out that we are the injured one and develop expectations of being looked after and protected. This can hinder our journey to doing more things we want to. Living in this fear affects our relationships, our sense of place in the world, and our ability to reach beyond our comfort zone to assist others. We search for a narrative that makes sense and removes threats, which doesn't always mean stretching out to connect with those outside the tribe.

Maybe we aren't looking outside ourselves to what we can do for other members of the tribe, because we are conserving resources for ourselves, because we're trying to survive, because phones, trauma, and FOMO have activated our survival mode.

If people are indeed activated in this fight or flight existence, some behaviours can be demonstrated that aren't conducive for connection. Aggression, defensiveness, seeming lack of thought or consideration, victim style language, diminished compassion, increased exhaustion… So, when we come across challenging scenarios, it would do us good to remember this. Sometimes those who should be a friend may seem like an enemy. Perhaps someone showing these signs is perceiving themselves as the injured of the flock. They're going through a really tough time. Maybe just like you.

If we become aware of this within ourselves, learn to calm our anxiety, even just a bit, we can start to look outside, think broader and bigger, and gaze across the horizon to see potential. It's not an easy feat, especially if we are pre-dispositioned to mental health challenges, or we develop them in tough times.

If we become aware of this in others, we can understand why people are the way they are. We don't have to tolerate and be subject to aggressive and unhealthy behaviour, but at least we can process it with a different lens. They must find their path to overcoming the overwhelm of big feelings and learn ways to not let it leak out so much that it hurts people. We can manage our own responses and boundaries, ensuring we do all we can in our own lives to offer a kind and connected demeanor to the world.

Connection is a crazy vehicle on a wild right through this mortal coil. Jump on board!

There are many stories of people overcoming their crises and achieving all they want to in life. There are many ways to manage and live with anxiety, depression, and accept these dark parts of ourselves. We kind of need to trick our brains. We front up to the darkness and become curious about it. When we dig a little deeper, we can see that intentions of various parts of ourselves are often good, but we have fought with ourselves for so long, it can be hard to undo the patterns. But it's possible.

We should show kindness to the things we struggle with the most. The anxiety, the fight and flight, the trauma and even the phone addiction.

Instead, we fight with these things, try to hide them, or banish them altogether. We tousle with ourselves, living in perpetual self-loathing, and stuck on a merry go round of limitation. The irony being, that the love you offer to these hidden demons is likely to do the job we think war is needed for. It is the most counterintuitive thing to fight for peace. You want peace in the turmoil of your mind, then you must bring peace. Fighting against the parts of yourself you're at odds with only brings more carnage. Peaceful negotiation is where you'll find what you seek. Giving love to the shadow brings it into light, and its power is diffused.

I sometimes talk to myself:

"Oh, there you are fear. What are you telling me today?"

"Hey there, controlling self, you're at it again. How can I help you? What do you need?"

Kindness. KINDNESS. KIIINNNDDNEESSSSSS.

When we can catch even a hint of this and apply it in our lives, we can start to grow and reconnect in areas we didn't know we could. We can reach out and make choices that encourage and build ourselves and our relationships. We start to become more confident in ourselves and open pathways to relate to people. We begin to uncover the dreams we pushed so far down, because we hated ourselves too much to believe they could become real. Those dreams, those words, ideas, voices, that linger deep, and never leave you, no matter how much you silence them…maybe they're holding the way forward for you. Maybe that's your path to reconnection.

## ANCHORing our Connections

How do we develop relationships that grow? I've worked out a nifty little model that provides some ideas about fostering healthy connections.

# 11

## ACCEPTANCE of Self

*"I love you just the way you are..."*

—Billy Joel

The first aspect of anchoring your connections is acceptance of your SELF. If you are struggling with your self-worth and/or self-esteem, it's not a great foundation to be working from. You may overcompensate in relationships in order to please people. You might disconnect because you feel you aren't worthy of connection and love. There may be a number of barriers between you and healthy relationships. We talked about 'shitty behaviour' previously, so we know that the first step to recovery and repair is self-compassion.

DEEP self-acceptance. It's rewriting old scripts about who we are - accepting mistakes, embracing flaws.

Use everyday situations to understand who you are. Observing how you respond to certain events in life is the ultimate free education. Everything is a mirror if you'll let it be. But you might find you don't like who you see in the mirror when challenges with people arise.

I realised in more recent years that I'm actually quite an intense person with really big feelings, strong ideas and I can get a bit of a rant on. I realized that somewhere along the way, and I'd been trying to hide that. I didn't like it about myself, and obviously others hadn't too, because I developed quite the suite of coping mechanisms to mask myself. I realised that I was trying to be someone more likeable ALL the time, and the parts of me that I tried to hide, I didn't really like very much. Ouch.

How exactly do you learn to like and accept yourself?

Firstly, read Part 1. Get to know yourself. All the parts of you. And you must understand that you are more than 1 thing. There are many parts of you. Some you'll loathe, as you get to know them, you'll learn to love them. Give them grace, compassion, ask them what they want. That part of you that is angry and aggressive is just a part that has needs. What are it's needs? Turn towards it and find out!

"Hey anger, I see you. What is it that you need? What is it that's getting you so riled up?"

You didn't show up here unlikeable. Most people are OK with babies. We just learned some things along the way that made us behave in a certain way. Maybe we had trauma… (probably).

So, I'm learning to like myself by turning towards all those parts of me. I'm learning to offer love, compassion, and kindness to all the versions of Jade that have existed, holy Jesus there has been a few (pun directed at anyone who knows one of my past lives was as an evangelical Christian). I had to learn to not be angry at the young me I perceived to be a stupid girl who got duped into a toxic religious organisation.

This is what I've learned from my therapy. All the parts of yourself are worthy of love. The hurt and angry parts. The childlike parts. The silly parts. The unusual parts. They all just need love and attention through the lens of compassion, forgiveness, acceptance. Maybe you didn't get that love from those random people you ended up with, or maybe your parents loved you immensely, it's still possible to like, love and care for yourself more.

Just be with YOU. Be proud of yourself. Be OK with being sad or mad. It's normal to feel things. You're allowed to have an opinion, boundaries, a strong instinct about something.

There's a reason WHY you have adapted or covered up or behave in a certain way. Don't be so hard on yourself for your mistakes and things that are hard to change.

If your behaviours are destructive to yourself or others, and you find it hard to stop, please, find some help.

You can't change WHO YOU ARE. So, you have to learn to live with yourself, create the best version of you, and share that with others.

# 12

## NON-JUDGMENT of Others

*"That's the thing with anger, it begs to stick around,
so it can fleece you of your beauty…"*

—Sam Fender

This kind of acceptance IS about the other person. We are in no position to be casting judgment on other people's stuff.

What is being judgmental? We are judgmental of people when we believe someone should be making choices in a different way, behaving differently, should have the same kind of values as us, aren't 'up to standard' in some way.

Being judgmental is also making assumptions about people, coming to conclusions about them and their lives, and preempting how they might behave or even think about you.

I realised that my default position of 'people don't like me' was me being absolutely judgmental. I would often approach business gatherings this way, feeling like I'm so different that people will not understand or like me. I didn't even realise it, but barriers would go up, and I obviously can't get the best out of a social situation if I'm making judgments on people before we've even engaged! It came as a surprise that my own insecurities and trauma were really ruining opportunities for me. My self-protection was actually being very poisonous.

Being truly non-judgmental is accepting people as they are, without imposing our preconceived notions or biases onto them. When we shed the cloak of judgment, we allow others to be their authentic selves, creating an environment of trust.

We can do our best to demonstrate this, and generate a space for openness, but how others approach life is something we have zero control over. If we have built mutual respect and trust, there may be some influence towards changing someone, but unless we are really close to a person, we know very little about what is going on for them.

Is it hard to reserve judgment? You bet! I am very critical about other drivers when I'm driving a car, and even get judgy over people who are judgy. But how I work towards being non-judgmental is by accepting that humans are just human, understanding there are many factors that influence people's choices, and having compassion that what you see isn't the full picture of them as a person. (Of course, when it comes to serious crimes, there's a different viewpoint, but I'm talking generally about the folks we spend time with day to day.)

We are wired to categorise people, identify what is different and seek out what is similar. It's probably an out-of-date survival safety mechanism. But I think this instinctive pattern gets in the way of what could be more positive and fulfilling interactions.

A part of being non-judgmental is forgiveness. These virtues will most certainly level up your relationships, and the following easy tips will show you how!

I'm kidding. Forgiveness doesn't usually happen easily, no matter how good my tips are.

But as jokey as I get about it, focused effort on these things has helped my life immensely. Forgiving misgivings isn't really for the benefit of others, it's really about what it does for YOU.

I find that people can be a bit annoying. You probably have the same problem. Even if we don't talk about it, it's normal to get agitated, angry, frustrated with other humans.

There are so many things that people do that grind our gears. Perhaps you've filled someone's bucket generously and they haven't reciprocated. Perhaps they've got an oppositional opinion about something important to you, and they aren't open to a mature discourse about it. Perhaps they acted like a dick at Christmas time. Maybe you called THEM the last 4 times, and they haven't taken their turn to be in touch. Maybe they're just always late. Maybe you had a fist fight at a party. There are many opportunities to feel angry.

When these feelings come up, it usually it means a boundary has been crossed, a value has been compromised, or we simply just don't agree on something. It's what you do with that frustration and anger that counts. If we are impulsive with these feelings and allow them to explode without taking a beat, it can be very harmful and destructive for everyone involved. If we allow them to stew and then talk shit about people behind their backs, it's like poison for our souls.

Here's the thing, let yourself feel the feelings, but don't stay in them.

The feelings themselves aren't negative, it's what we choose to do with them that can be scary and upsetting and uncomfortable. Anger can lead to violence. Frustration can lead to yelling. Disappointment can lead to the silent treatment. That's why we're afraid of these things. The consequences of the feelings are what we're uncomfortable with. It's the lack of control people seem to have when they occur. What if we practiced controlling them? First, acceptance, but what about actively DECIDING what to do with it.

Forgiveness is not putting yourself back into a situation where your boundaries can be crossed again. It's not 'letting someone off the hook'. It's a process of what YOU choose to do with your own response to someone else's actions.

PART 2 - OTHERS

What actions will YOU take to protect yourself from the long-term damage of hard feelings?

Of course, you are really self-aware now that you've read part 1 of this book, you'll know to give yourself some space to observe. Just, take a breath, examine your feelings, and ask yourself WHY you're irritated, angry, upset, and then figure out how to move forward. Moving through the emotions means not fighting with the feelings that come up, but also not fighting with people around you. This could take half an hour; it might take three years to process the emotions of hurtful events. Violence is no good, so if you're getting to that point I suggest removing yourself. Yelling at someone, while not super healthy, is going to happen, but I also suggest being aware enough to know when walking away is the best solution.

## Activity - Black Smoke

*Here's an exercise. Imagine your hard feelings as a little cloud of black smoke. The anger, annoyance, whatever the emotion is.*

*Imagine it inside you. Swirling around, creating these very real vibes in your body and mind.*

*Now, scientifically, a cloud can transform. Some clouds transform into liquid and then crystal. So what you want to do is let it turn to liquid, and make its way out of your system. You don't want it to get to a crystallised point, because then it becomes a bit sharp, and takes up unnecessary space. Don't let this cloud take up space in your soul for very long. Because the more those black clouds end up as crystals in your soul, the less room there is for light and air. Then you'll find yourself being unable to breathe, clogged up, and there will be more work in chipping away at the dark crystals in your soul. It's much easier to process and release it earlier, when maybe it comes out in your sweat, or your wee, or if you need to, vomit, spit whatever. It's a real thing, get it out of your system!*

Yes, I did just suggest you could vomit up your unforgiveness. Thanks for coming to my TED talk. Non-judgment and forgiveness are closely intertwined, and inherent to the acceptance of other humans just being how they are - flawed and unpredictable. Coming to this place can help in your closest relationships, and with the incidental interactions that happen in daily life.

I don't believe forgiveness is a ticket to opening up all your boundaries. It's much more about what YOU do with your own feelings, than what nice platitudes you offer someone who has done you wrong. People can be real dicks, and sometimes there is just no place for that in our lives. Keep firm in your own personal values, create boundaries to protect yourself and your loved ones, and work on dissolving that black smoke in your own personal ritual.

There are most definitely some horrible hurtful things that people do to us, and awful life stuff that happens. I mean that's what this book is supposed to be helping you with. So, if this brings up something serious, please reach out to your healthcare professional. I believe we all could use a little (or a lot of) therapy.

# 13

## COMPASSION for People

> *"Purge the soul*
> *Make love your goal"*
>
> —Frankie Goes to Hollywood

Compassion isn't pity. Pity is just distanced disempowerment. Compassion is also different to empathy. Where empathy is more about feeling emotions on behalf of someone, compassion is love in action. It's the bridge between our hearts and the world around us. It's thinking beyond your own problems and acknowledging the problems others might have. It's celebrating with people when they have a win, no matter what that same thing would mean to you. It's taking actions to support someone in their life, even if you don't feel the same emotions they do about a situation.

Reflecting on my own interactions with people, I've discerned three distinct modes of engagement:

1. **FEARFUL:** I am at times, scared of people. I often find myself feeling 'less than' and seeking approval or validation, and as I previously talked about, making judgments about whether people 'like me or not'. This

usually happens if I'm in that fight or flight state, feeling anxious, unsafe, or in a brand new situation.

2. **IRATE:** I get mad as hell, but generally when I'm driving. Strangers seem so idiotic on the roads. I also get really mad when people do mean and inconsiderate stuff.

3. **CURIOUS and COMPASSIONATE:** This is the nicest place to be obviously but can be the hardest position to take at times. It's space for acceptance, understanding that people just do people stuff, and we are all in this together.

I'm working on all of these, obviously aiming to mostly be in number three. Being autistic and ADHD, it's kind of hard to regulate emotions. They happen so fast and deep sometimes, it's challenging to manage. Maybe you experience the same thing - big feelings and fast responses?

It's ok that it happens. I just figure we have limited time in this life, so dwelling in the fear or anger doesn't really serve us well. There's no point staying mad about anything really. It definitely doesn't help in the pursuit of a connected and fulfilling life to hold on to anger. People mightn't realise that I'm kind of an angry person underneath all my Zen. (lol). Sometimes I feel like there is a lot to get mad about. For example, war is totally ridiculous, there's totally enough money in existence to help the more vulnerable people and set up better systems, cutting in line is pretty rude, but I can't live from these frustrations. I have to accept that they exist and do my best to bring something to the world that counteracts the anger-inducing ways of the world.

The resolution I have found is to try and live from that place of curiosity and compassion. People are infinitely interesting, with myriad of reasons why they do all the things they do. It's fascinating! We live in complex world, with complex immediate situations, and as I've talked about, I think we're just generally too overloaded and our brains sometimes malfunction.

We don't always have conscious control over how we react, so we can't expect others to be any better. Compassion becomes all the more vital for understanding each other's missteps every time we leave the house. There inevitably comes a moment when we ourselves need compassion, and by extending it to others, we sow the seeds of a more compassionate world.

In the grand scheme of building relationships, compassion is the glue that binds us together. It can be a force for good, to help us in the midst of misunderstanding and miscommunication. When we choose compassion, we're choosing to see beyond the surface, to understand the layers beneath what might be going on for another human.

I've found that the more I strive to be in that curious and compassionate state, the more fulfilling my relationships become. It's akin to uncovering hidden treasure within the hearts of others. It's definitely not the easiest path, opening yourself up to vulnerability, giving more of a shit about people and issues, and being OK with things you might've disagreed with in the past. It's about letting go of judgment and embracing understanding, surely this has an impact not only on our personal relationships, but also the broader world around us?

# 14

## HONESTY is the Best Policy

*"I'm a different person."*

—The Shapeshifters

Being vulnerable is to show another person that you are human. Vulnerability is a key ingredient in connection. Sharing honestly with people helps you be authentic and gives permission for others to be vulnerable too. When we see the real parts of each other, it's easier to blend them in some way. Being real brings connection, but I know this is very hard for some people. We experience hurt and trauma and build walls and personas to protect our real selves from being seen. I'd been doing it for years.

There is obviously a risk of being hurt or rejected when you share truth. But the reward is in you making the best contribution to connection that you possibly can. If someone rejects the 'real' you, then you know you don't need to continue spending energy there.

There is honesty in the sense of our personal selves, sharing our identity in an authentic way and being vulnerable with our emotions, but there is also honesty in the subject of lying.

It didn't immediately occur to me to think and talk about lying, because I think that people are generally honest, like I try to be.

What I was reminded of though, is that there are different kinds of lies. You know, I lie to the GP about how many drinks I have per week, but I try to be honest about everything else.

There are lies we tell others to:

- make ourselves seem better than we think we are.
- cover up mistakes... to make ourselves seem better than we think we are.
- get something we want, like material things or power... to make ourselves seem better than we think we are.

Lying may just be a sign of low self-esteem. I actually used to lie a lot as a kid. I made up many elaborate stories about giants living in the forest, and a boyfriend I had who lived far away. I would lie to cover up my 'bad' behaviours and make myself seem better than I felt like I was. It didn't really go down that well. Kids were onto me.

This ADHD and autistic brain of mine had created masks and camouflage to try and fit in better. Having this understanding of myself makes so much sense as to why I lied as a child. I don't fabricate elaborate stories anymore, but I do have all this work to do in taking off the coping mechanisms I adopted. A process of what's called 'unmasking' in the neurodiverse space.

There were ways that I presented myself in order to feel safer, which include making up stories, mimicking others' behaviours, observing life for cues on how I should behave, speak and think. Because somewhere along the line as a kid, I showed up as myself, and it wasn't received well. I struggled with being bullied at school, and I struggled relationally at home. So, adapting myself was essential. It really ended up as a mish mash of a personality, I did not have good confidence as a kid and that still plagues me.

Lying is also a sign of self-betrayal. There must be dishonesty going on with the self if there is dishonesty with others. If you're in the habit of lying, to get out of it, you have to start with self-compassion.

Healthy adults who are doing the work and healing their wounds don't have a need to lie. They've started a process of being honest with themselves about the hard things, they've turned towards the hidden things, and aren't hindering their true self from emerging by hiding behind protective mechanisms.

Those earlier fibbing parts of me played a key role in keeping me safe, but now I have to allow my healed, healthier self to come forward, one step at a time. It's pretty scary to start letting your true self shine, but what a relief.

We can't expect genuine connection with people if we are a) lying to ourselves b) hiding our true self or c) overtly lying to other people.

Honesty is like freedom. Being open. True.
It's a weight off the chest.
It's an invitation to your tribe.
It's a portal to a new existence.

# 15

## OPENNESS with Others

*"Lean on me
When you're not strong
And I'll be your friend"*

—Bill Withers

This is really about listening. Listening, not to speak your part, but to engage, actually hear and comprehend what people are saying, and to respond. We're often pretty eager to say our piece and can have closed ears until we get to. This aspect of developing connection is about being curious, interested, allowing the energy and interests of another human be important to you. It's not just a technique repeating back to someone what they've said to show understanding. It's the thread of openness, the art of truly listening. In a world bustling with noise and opinions, the act of listening, is a subtle superpower, one that holds the potential to bridge gaps and nurture a deeper understanding of one another.

When you're in conversation, are you truly engaged in the exchange, or is your mind already jumping to the next steps of your response? We've all been there. We all have stories to tell, experiences to share, and viewpoints to defend. Yet, how often do we pause to let another person's narrative resonate within us?

"Active listening" is a term we've probably all heard. But it's more than just jargon; it's a conscious choice to immerse ourselves in the story of another. Think about the last time you really felt heard. Remember the warmth of that connection, the spark of genuine interest in someone else's words. Like being invited to sit around a campfire and your stories being welcomed. That's the power of active listening.

Yet, why does it seem like such a struggle? Is it our instinctive need to be heard, to assert our presence in a noisy world? Is it another survival tactic?

Openness isn't just about sharing your own stories—it's about creating a space where someone else's story can also unfold. The essence of everything we're talking about here, is communication. Transactions between humans to share messages, stories, experiences, and emotions is essential for our growing relationships. The landscape of how we interact has changed so drastically with the speedy rise of technology over the last two decades. Now we communicate via comments and likes, comedic videos and showcasing life's highlight reels. Getting real with one another is just not as common, and our reduced attention spans have surely reduced our ability to listen IRL.

Listening is an act of respect, a tribute to the uniqueness of every individual's journey.

There's a magic in quietening that internal chatter and allowing your open heart to invite vulnerability, not only from the speaker but also within yourself.

You're acknowledging that your understanding is a work in progress, that the world is far more nuanced than we usually pay attention to.

Can we allow space for those who need it, calling ourselves out when we feel the impatience rise?

Can we slow down enough to remember that we are all people, and we all need to feel seen, heard and understood? It can be so interesting to delve into the story of another person, and it helps you find YOUR people!

By cultivating the art of listening, by being curious and truly open to the stories and perspectives of others, we embrace a richer existence. Openness and listening are key ingredients to anchoring your connections and building understanding on a pathway to a more connected world.

# 16

## *RELATIONSHIPS for a Connected Life*

> *"But, oh, to get involved in the exchange*
> *Of human emotions*
> *Is ever so, ever so satisfying"*
>
> —Bjork

That intangible connection you've created with another human is always a relationship of sorts. You know that. And as I keep banging on about, I've come to realize that the journey of building relationships begins within ourselves. Our ability to truly connect with others mirrors our capacity to connect with our own selves.

Certain relationships are just about maintenance. Remember the Time/Love Model from Chapter 9? The ones that come up in the Friendly Strangers might be about maintenance. It might be workmates, in-law family, extended friend groups, school parents, or people in your sphere that you have pleasant times with, and are connected to, but don't have a growing relationship with. Now, the groups I have just mentioned may also contain some amazing soul connections! Don't get me wrong. But you perhaps can't expect fantastic genuine new friendships from all these places.

In a maintenance relationship, you might have regular contact, but you might never really talk real talk. It might be functional and logistical communication, it might be situational chit-chat, or small talk and pleasantries. These people can still be really important in your life, and it's possible to have long lovely friendships this way. We can't have soul connections with every person!

Sometimes the maintenance is bare minimum contact, frustrations in between, facades, pleasantries, but no real connection. We probably all have something like this going on, perhaps with family members. Because we expect more from family than other humans, we can be more frequently disappointed. So, it becomes protected, defensive, and prickly, from all sides.

We might keep things very surface level because it might not feel safe to be more vulnerable.

Maintenance relationships might break with conflict, or they might fade into the distance.

In any case, we want to have at least some fulfilling relationships that have growth and genuine connection.

There's a difference between growing relationships and maintenance relationships.

The tension comes when we expect the growing relationship to come from maintenance people, and if we have a maintenance relationship with people we expect to have a growing relationship with.

We might think building a growing relationship is about regular contact. But that's not the whole picture. Frequent chats don't necessarily mean we've got a strong, flourishing relationship with someone. We could have regular contact that is disconnected, disingenuous, and sometimes painful. We have regular contact with colleagues, but we don't stay in touch with all of them when we move jobs. We have regular contact with our baristas, but do you even know their name?

The real building happens in connection, and real connection transcends time and the human shell we live in.

I recently reconnected with a best friend from high school on email. She's one of those smart people who never got caught up in social media, or the fad of 'friending' your old high school pals just for stalking and not talking. We met up in real life, and both were teary to see each other after 18 years. We just connected. There's relationship there. Even if we don't see each other, or even keep in touch that often, there is a bond shared that creates relationship. That old saying of 'picking up where we left off' is how we describe this kind of connection.

The thing about relationship is the threads of our souls have been intertwined. It might sound a bit woo-woo, so let me explain in Brené Brown terms. Real relationship requires real talk and vulnerability. It's about shared values, a common bond, an intangible tie. Vulnerability is the platform for meaningful connection and a growing relationship.

If I am not being real, and the person across from me is not being real, then how do our souls find each other? When we hide ourselves, we rob ourselves of opportunity to connect on purpose. There is nothing more beautiful to me, than the real version of you, connecting to the real version of me. It literally brings tears to my eyes. To me THIS is the meaning of life, and it's so rare.

Growing relationships have moments like this frequently, bonds are created, you get to know each other and then you continue to accept each other as you morph into the next version of yourself.

Growing relationships use conflict as an opportunity for just that… growth. To move together towards solutions when tensions arise. They are communicative, have history, jokes, depth, and an intangible magic.

The real foundations of relationships are the things I've talked about: Acceptance, Non-judgment, Compassion, Honesty, and Openness. We can bring the best version of ourselves by embracing this stuff. Conflict and hard feelings will happen. Friendships come and go. We'll get agitated and hurt and frustrated along the way, but nothing beats genuine connection when we deliberately show up for others.

# 17

## Showing Up

*"We'll find out what we're made of
When we are called to help our friends in need"*

—Bruno Mars

Sometimes we are tired and burned out and feel like there isn't much to give. We do have to know our own boundaries. When I was going through these really hard times, people sometimes said to me that they wanted to help but didn't know how.

And on the flip side, I have received incredible support from dear friends and family through the most difficult times in my life. Unfortunately, some people disappear completely, as I'm sure I've done myself.

We are conditioned to accept people conditionally. Fit, healthy, working, and wealthy are often the qualities we look for, probably quite subconsciously. It's sort of a primal thing I think. These attributes are definitely attractive, and many of us would rather stick with people who display them than tend to the weaker ones in the herd who are challenged and suffering. But HELLO!? We are meant to be evolved, and I think evolved means being empathetic, being able to override our primal tendencies, and tap into a higher self. A self that sees beyond scarcity and is able to share and show up for people in our lives when they aren't looking so fit, healthy, working or wealthy. There are so many situations that impact this. Times when we really need each other:

- Having a baby.
- Going through illness, medical procedures and diagnoses.
- Mental illness episodes.
- Being a carer for someone with illness or disability.
- Job loss.
- Financial trouble.
- Moving house.
- Separation and divorce.
- Death in the family.
- Challenges with kids or family.

Plus, the many other things that come up in our lives…so I created a guide on ways to show up. These are some ideas about things we can do for each other, when we feel like we want to help but don't know how, but importantly, when we have the capacity to. If we're conscious of our boundaries, energy levels, and have our own needs met, then perhaps there's some space for a few extra things we can do for one another.

# PRACTICAL WAYS TO SHOW UP:

**The Showing Up Mantra**
*If someone I care about is going through something hard, I'm going to show up, in whatever way I know how.*

Send a text. This literally takes 3.2 seconds. "I'm thinking of you."

Even better, be honest if you feel awkward, and say "I know you're going through a tough time; I don't actually know what I can do. But I'm thinking of you. Is there anything you need?"

Make a phone call. If you're like me, you might avoid real-life phone conversations because we just don't communicate that way anymore. But it's still a good thing to do to let someone know you're thinking of them.

Offer to take the kids to school or pick them up.

Send another text.

Make a meal. People often make food for tough times, and that is fabulous. But it might be nice to stagger it and check how much capacity their freezer has. It's one of the loveliest and simplest gestures.

Handwrite a card.

Make a nice comment on their social media post.

Organise a cleaner. Find out what day of the week suits and organise someone to come along and help with some things around the house. What a treat!

Write a letter and send it in the mail. I have a friend who does this for no real reason at all, and it is the most delightful thing.

Cook some baking. Biscuits and treats are nice with a cup of tea in the afternoon.

Do grocery shopping. Get a few basics and bring them over or send them via delivery!

Go over and fold laundry. Who wouldn't want that? You're basically my friend forever if you could just sort out my kids' clothes.

Organise to take the kids to a movie. Straightforward, fun for you, and helpful for parents.

Invite them around to your house. It feels like years since being invited anywhere for dinner was a thing. And to be fair I haven't really cooked for anyone either. Do people just not do that anymore?

Buy them some magazines. Something interesting and relevant to what they like. Photography, or music, or interiors, or puzzle books!

PART 2 - OTHERS

Pay for their Netflix subscription. I mean, I don't know if you can do it directly, but you can offer a sum of cash that would cover a streaming service for a few months.

Send memes and funny messages. Again, super easy, and entertaining. Laughter is like medicine.

Send some flowers. Or a plant. A special little succulent is a nice idea for someone who may not like to look after plants.

Make a piece of art. Do you build or paint, or crochet? Make a little something. It's such a kind and meaningful thing to do.

Write a story for them. Maybe a cute short story with them as the superhero!

Shout them a holiday. That's a big one, but you could rally up a few people to make it happen, or if you've got the cash, what better way to share it?

Remember appointment times and message them beforehand or after.

Go over and do some Marie Kondoing. Ask what part of the house your pal needs a hand with and help them chuck some junk or organise some drawers.

135

Get tickets to something special. A theatre show, or a gig, something they'd enjoy a night out doing.

Take wine and cheese over. What a lovely thing to do on a Friday afternoon. "Hey, I'm gonna bring wine and cheese to your house!"

Find out more about their condition and talk about it. I know this meant a lot to me when someone told me they had looked up Chiari Malformation, it showed me they were interested and cared. And on that…

Really listen when they talk about what's going on. If you have regular conversations, ask about specific things to do with what they've told you. This is true communication.

Make a checklist of podcasts they can listen to while recovering.

Buy them and set up an audible book service.

Make them a Spotify playlist.

Get them a cool t-shirt made.

Crowdsource some gift vouchers for groceries or petrol.

Visit them in the hospital!

Send a message, especially when you aren't sure. ALWAYS send the message.

Be consistent and regular with your contact if you're a close loved one committed to their journey. Connection is the platform for healing, and if you're a nearest or dearest, you are kinda obligated. So, get in there with your kind gestures and messages.

Be honest about your own feelings, share that you're feeling busy or overwhelmed in your own life, but you care about them. I'm thinking about grief when I say this, but please be careful not to pour out your own big feelings onto someone who has lost someone close.

Pick them up and drive them to a massage appointment you've made for them.

Send money gifts! Money is always welcome if you can't do something in person or can't think of something, or don't have much time.

Write a poem.

Make a video instead of a text message! So personal and fun.

Buy them a set of fresh new sheets! Especially pertinent if they're having a time of being bed ridden.

Book a day of fun in for when they're recovered. "I'm going to pick you up and take you on a day trip to somewhere cool. Have brunch, a nature walk, or go to the gallery. "

Take them away on a weekend retreat. A yoga retreat, meditation camp, there are always events on.

Gather some friends and visit for dinner.

Hugs! Did you know that hugging for 20 seconds or longer generates serotonin, dopamine, and other benefits for the body and mind? Please get consent.

Ask them what they need. But most people struggle with asking for help, so offer a few different options you can do, and see what they say.

Be a coordinator while they're in hospital or going through their challenge. If you've got a few friends you know would be able to help, be the person who collects things together for your buddy.

Buy their coffee for a week at their favourite cafe as a surprise. When they go to order, it's already taken care of!

Send a stripper or a singing telegram! It might be just the thing that's needed.

Collect money with others and get a special voucher for something they love.

Send premade meals to be delivered for a couple of weeks.

Take some rum balls or other boozy or fun food.

Start a go fund me page to help with bills.

Make a care package with a collection of helpful items.

Buy a set of things to encourage creativity. Nice paper and pens, or some paints or pastels, or a journal.

Bake a really elaborate and beautiful cake for them for no reason at all.

It takes about 2 seconds to send a meme or gif or a message. Do that again.

Be proactive when working out logistics. Everyone's brain is tired, but it's especially hard when you're sick, or struggling with mental health during crisis time. Offer a time, place, and suggestions for engagements. It's one of the main barriers to connecting is thinking about the logistics of getting together. Making decisions FOR people might seem presumptuous, but it gives a solid start. "Hey, are you free to meet at Cool Place on Tuesday at 10 a.m. I'd really like to take you there."

Most people we know are going through something, and we all have our own stuff too. It's impossible to show up for everyone, but if we can even do little things for a couple of people, it makes a world of difference.

# 18

## *Balancing the Buckets*

*"I would rather starve than eat your bread"*

—Pearl Jam

Friendships are dynamic. Sometimes they are exhausting, uncomfortable, or even recognisably toxic.

One of the big questions is "How do I know when it's time to move on or let go?"

It's tricky. Sometimes this just happens naturally, and sometimes it's about the need for boundaries. And it deserves a little chapter section to discuss.

Firstly, if you've been through Part 1 - Yourself, then you'll have an idea of what your values are, which will give you a sense of your boundaries. You'll know when a line has been crossed because one of your values will be compromised.

For example, if one of your values is integrity, and someone lies to you, you will feel pretty strongly about that.

Some people talk about being generous and giving without expecting anything in return, and I get that. For example, I give regularly to some charity organisations, and I don't expect anything in return from them. The return for me is knowing that I'm sharing some of my privilege, which to me is just the right thing to do. I believe in generosity as a core value. However, I also believe there is a need for transactions in relationships.

When it comes to individuals, there's a way I look at this.
The idea of balanced buckets.
Where there's an investment into each other's buckets, it creates a transactional energy between you in a relationship.

You put something (theoretical) into someone's bucket, and you might do that many times. If they don't put much back into yours, you might feel like there's an imbalance in the relationship. This can cause frustration.

Sometimes I feel like I make the majority of the effort to organise catch-ups with certain people. So, I stop doing it, and then they might never respond again. Well, that tells you something, doesn't it? I was giving energy that didn't get reciprocated in that relationship, and then it dissipated. It was a one-sided transaction.

Some people might only want to do activities on THEIR terms, and you meet those terms.

That might be OK for a while, but when the flexibility isn't returned, it feels like you've lost out somehow.

It's different for different types of relationships. If it's a mentoring relationship, it might be appropriate that you meet that person who is helping you, wherever they want. Because they're giving back to you in a different way.

I think perhaps people get annoyed in relationships and don't know why. I think it's because of this imbalance in the bucket investment.

If you've invested enough into someone's bucket, and you make a mistake, there's energy to cover it. If you haven't invested much, you've taken too much, and you breach a boundary or two, well, don't be surprised if things start to crumble.

The way my neurodivergent, supercharged empathetic brain works, is that I find much more meaning in relationships than some other people do. I am highly sensitive, seek connection as a major priority, and deal with rejection very stressfully. So, I try really hard to make relationships, friendships, and connections work with people. I expect a lot, often more than what is possible, and in the past that may have come across as weird or obsessive. I tend to avoid small talk, get deep quickly, and respond to people with (what I think are) relatable stories about myself as a way of connecting.

This can be a bit intense, and it's taken me many years to realise this about myself. What I've also learned is how people respond to attempts at connection. Those who are open and similar to me, appreciate the way I approach conversations and relationship building, others who are different, might not reply as frequently to digital communication or need to spend as much time connecting.

It takes a lot for me to pull back on kindness, energy or friendship. And to be fair, I'm not that good at having open conversations when I feel like something isn't working. My signal tends to be a reduction in investment. I love the relationships where there is a natural balancing of the buckets. You know those connections where it isn't hard work, you know when it's time to invest, and when there's enough in the bucket for you to cancel a plan.

*"You're barking up the wrong tree."*

This sentence changed the way I perceived my efforts. As harsh as it sounds, someone said this to me when I was complaining to them about people I had been trying very hard to connect with and weren't responding in the way that I hoped for. It was such a freeing moment, to realise that the need for a connection I had was not going to be filled by this person/people, and I had to fill my cup elsewhere. My people are probably in another tree.

What a revelation!

Fear creeps in though...What if I can't find the right tree? What happens if I let go of trying so hard to connect with people? I often have strong feelings of being rejected and alone in the world. It's not true, I have a lot of amazing people in my life, but the sense of this can be very overwhelming and real.

Changing my expectations around relationships has helped me manage some of this emotional turmoil. Instead of replaying interactions from years ago, putting too much onus on what should just be short-term connections, and expecting others to want to engage with me in the same way. I have learned that not every person I meet should be super important to me, and how to have a better perspective about the nature of relationships. Not everyone is like this, of course.

It can take time to find your people. Sometimes finding your SELF first will help you find your people (See Part 1.) And mapping out your Love/Time relationship model will help you sort out where to spend your energy. (See Chapter 9)

Sometimes you're lucky enough to easily stumble into people you resonate with, people that make you realise who YOU are, help you feel safe, and they support you in discovering your qualities. If you do find someone in this world who celebrates you, someone who tells others about how amazing you are, someone who gives you space to be you, hold on to them. Invest in their bucket, they are probably investing into yours, and what a healing, edifying beautiful thing to have in this god forsaken life!

# PART 3 - LIFE

# 19

## *Part 3 Introduction - Life, Absurd Life*

*"Life oh life, oohhhh life"*

—Desiree

All this... It's just made up stuff.

We just happen to be here, at this time of late-stage capitalism, when some particular people got a lucky break and are having a turn to rule the world.

Empires have happened before, and they'll happen again. But as we can see, there is change happening, and soon, it will be someone else's turn to rule, with THEIR made-up stuff. And that will have good and bad, and then the next empire will do it. And we'll all just keep going around in circles and never reach this utopia we've all be conditioned to believe in. Probably because the world is likely to implode first.

It might all just feel like a sick joke at times, but we have to make the best of it. And try to find the funny side when we can.

It stuns me that not everyone sits around wondering what the hell we are doing here inside these meat sacks. Feeling pain, enjoying chocolate mousse, and making hard decisions. What IS this?!

Lots of people seem fine with ignoring that gnawing feeling, or they don't even have one. They just, exist. Quite happily, not even wondering for a second, WHY? Disappointingly, for most people, purpose isn't found in a cereal box or under the couch, nor does it appear as a bolt of lightning.

If you are a bit like me, and grapple with the confusion of existence, here is what I think one answer is:

We make our own WHY. It's a D I WHY. Get it?

Dad joke. But I think we just have to make our own meaning out of our lives.

In an existentialist nightmare, I struggle with this on a daily basis. So if I had to boil it down, my meaning is just, to be the truest, best version of me, and hope that I can help some people along the way.

Yours might be different, more specific, or you mightn't care at all about having much meaning to life. You mightn't want to cast your brain much further than yourself and those you love. Some people don't, and that's cool.

I can't keep my gaze so near. I can't help but to have a broader view of the context of life. I think big, and my brain engages in broad exploration. Seeing those patterns, collecting all that data, trying to make sense of things. I don't know that I've figured much out, this world is so complex. But I've noticed a couple of things, through my journey. And I loved rambling about this shit. So, if you like to think bigger picture, join me for a chat about the context we're in. As I observe, from a place of neurodivergence and reasonable privilege in modern Australia.

Remember COVID? How many people were excited at the thought the world might turn into a more caring friendly place? There was hope that the collective experience we had would draw us together, creating new systems that we might live a more contented, less busy and rushed life. We thought it all might change - which it has, but not necessarily in the ways we thought. It hasn't really drawn us closer to the utopian dream of peace and harmony for all. Somehow, I felt like it got slightly more fractured, and the systems we are subject to are stronger than ever. How about that inflation and housing crisis huh?

I know of people who felt abandoned and betrayed by vaccines and government decisions, and then abandoned their own loved ones in vehement disagreement. I can see both sides of the argument, but don't really dig the division. Somehow, the rich got richer, company profits and property prices soared and people started fleeing their offices or decided to leave their jobs altogether.

The cost of living has skyrocketed, creating all kinds of social and economic problems. There are challenges in this world that we will never find solutions for, and I guess we must come to an acceptance of this. At least, that is what I am aiming to do.

I remember feeling quite dissociated coming out of what was a comparatively short lockdown, nervous, and uncertain, and I don't think I was the only one. It took some time to re-socialise. To reconnect. To build up energy and work out how to be in society again. Are we closer? More united? I don't know. We do have collective experiences to reflect on, but we all seem to perceive it differently.

Whether that particular trauma played any part in a more caring and united world or not, what we do know from that experience is that disconnection is unhealthy. It's way too easy to disconnect these days. We have those black rectangles in our hands that we can zone out and get lost inside.

How do we reconnect with life, with the big picture, with Earth?!

Moving from a place of existential crisis, into a fresh perspective of finding good things in life despite hard challenges requires that we look at the context of existence. Like the weirdo that I am, I can't help but ask WHY, and try to work it out. Looking at the bigger picture of the world and all that goes on, has helped me understand who I am, and how my perception of these somewhat intangible sociological influences impacts me on a day-to-day basis. So let's work through a collection of ideas, thoughts, and questions about life and consider why things are the way they are, and then dive into the Meaning Matrix to see where you might find meaning for your life.

Is this a bit political? Yes. Of course. Everything is.

# 20

## *Exploring Purpose*

*"All in all, there's something to give
All in all, there's something to do
All in all, there's something to live"*

—Air

If you've hung around with me long enough, you might have heard me ramble about the little parts of Maslow's Hierarchy of Needs pyramid, right at the top - Esteem and Self-Actualisation.

Once our other needs are met - Physiological, Safety, Love and Belonging, we get into this complex set of needs that seem to be exclusive to humans.

## MASLOW'S HEIRARCHY of NEEDS:

Attaining recognition for your skills and achievements, and living your highest potential, are, according to Maslow and others, actual human needs. NEEDS. And I think they have a lot to do with feeling purposeful in life.

Here's my interpretation of what this looks like:

**For Esteem...**
We need our bosses to tell us we're doing a good job.
We need the ceremonies that acknowledge achievement.
We need our partners to support and encourage us in our pursuits, whether they be home based, employment, recreation, business, etc.
We NEED some accolades and high fives.

**For Self-Actualisation...**
We need opportunities to demonstrate our skills, interests, and abilities.
We need to be challenged.
We need to embark on personal growth.
We need to see change in our lives.
We NEED to do things that we love doing to discover our fullest potential.

Nobody thrives doing work they hate.

It appears capitalism chopped off the top of the hierarchy, creating so many jobs that people loathe, using humans as slaves, and telling us that we should be grateful for the bare basics. Don't get me wrong, gratitude for having the basics of life is essential. However, some of the people trapped in this system don't even have that, and the gap is widening. Many folks in this world don't even have their basic needs met. I believe all humans have the right to not only that, but also to fulfill their potential, through whatever path makes that possible.

Some people know their calling from a young age, understanding exactly what their journey in life will be. Perhaps ALL their other needs were met from early on. Yay for them!

Some people take time to discover themselves, once they've worked at having all the other needs met because earlier life was a bit more challenging.

But it's all pretty hard to get up the pyramid if your basic needs aren't being met OR... you PERCEIVE your needs aren't being met.

It's sort of like you have to acknowledge and appreciate that your basic requirements are met if you have that privilege, and then you can start leveling up the hierarchy of needs. Gratitude proceeds growth.

What often comes up in this discussion about self is the notion of what you believe your purpose to be. So, let's take a moment to talk about that ever-elusive purpose.

Flowers know what they're supposed to do. Grow, be pretty, smell nice.

Lions know what they need to do. Hunt, survive, and relax knowing they are an apex predator.

Humans? Well, we rush around in a flurry of activities, hoping some lightning bolt will strike us with a grand gesture of bestowing purpose. Like Moses with his commandments up the hill, or waiting for a bus that never comes.

MAKING LEMONADE

*Why do I continuously look outside myself for meaning?*

Those lucky people who know exactly who they are and what they're meant to do, seem to navigate the life challenges with ease and strength. Some people don't even THINK about purpose, and what on earth they're here for. I find that delightful. Imagine not even caring much about it! Blissful ignorance? Yes, please! Do I just tell my overworking brain and emotions to STFU? Probably can't. So, for the rest of us floundering around wondering what to do next, it doesn't seem as straightforward.

Some people interchange 'purpose' with 'passion'. Find your PASSION. Well, you'll never be passionate about anything for a lifetime, it's more about finding what you can be patient with and running with that. It's more like....

*How much BS are you willing to put up with in order to follow a purposeful path that aligns with who you are?*

Someone asked me one day, "If I said you could have $5m but you could only live for one more day, what would you do?"

The cynical part said "Thank God. Get me out of this deteriorating flesh trap and off the face of this burning planet prison."

But I don't really mean it.

The fierce mother part of me says "I'll take the money, set my kids up for life, and have a nice final day drinking margaritas at the beach" With this option, in reality I think I'd be at a lawyer's office furiously dealing with all the paperwork as the clock ticks.

So, I don't really think that's a good option either.

I don't know what I would do, but it does make you think. I do actually want life. As much as wanting to give up has been part of my mental health journey, I'm an optimistic nihilist, and I want to see life through in a purposeful and meaningful way until the day I'm supposed to go. I want to find the limits of potential and reach the top of the self-actualizing pyramid. Circumstances can get really shitty, but I find there is always some light in them. Even if I can only see it retrospectively.

So then, what do I want to do with these days I have? If we get back to basics, what really matters? Working for the basic needs is just a baseline, fulfillment and growth also really, REALLY matter. That is the purpose. Pushing towards the edges of the potential that YOU have.

People say we get to choose, but not everyone can do exactly what they want. Choosing your life is privilege. As much as I talk about creating the life you want, and being proactive in your approach to living, we all have some limitations. That's the challenge, the fun, the adventure. Purpose is the meaning you make out of the circumstances you are in. Problem solving whatever is in front of you. Even if it's painful. Really, we just have to find the purpose of the next moment.

What's the next step?
What do I enjoy?
How can I connect with someone?
**What contribution can I make?**

When you know yourself, have a connection with people, and have considered the world beyond your own bubble, the answers to this question will become more apparent.

# 21

## *Living the Millennial Middle-Class Dream*

> *"And you may find yourself behind the wheel of a large automobile*
> *And you may find yourself in a beautiful house, with a beautiful wife*
> *And you may ask yourself, "Well, how did I get here?"*
>
> **—Talking Heads**

So, we talked about our personal patterns in part one, but there are also the broader patterns of society that we can observe and (try to) make sense of things.

I glean a lot of info from content and the media and sometimes will notice trends before they really pick up. Especially creative ones. Patterns in fashion, art, and music tell us a story of where humanity is at. Resurgences of past trends mean we're looking for something of the essence of that era. It happens all the time, reminiscing, nostalgia, recurrences.

They might seem innocuous, but right now in 2023 the longing for the early 2000's is coming through in low-rise baggy jeans and crop tops, in a refreshed popularity of pop music and celebrities from that era. Are we craving a less complicated time? A time right before screen time had taken up hours of our day, and when climate change was a distant threat and not right on our doorstep in the form of fire, flood and obscure unpredictable weather. I guess things seemed more fun back then, perhaps there's a longing for the perceived simplicity those years offered. Hindsight is a beautiful thing.

Obviously not every person rolls with this aspect of culture and starts busting out the low riders and chain belts with an emo fringe. It all changes and shifts as a layer within the broader societal norms. It emerges in pop culture, and with young people as they explore themselves. (I have two tweens who think it's awesome to play Backstreet Boys and Britney Spears). The arts, pop culture, entertainment turn over much faster than some of the institutionalised markers of our cultural flow.

There was a recent year of the Triple J Hottest 100 countdown where an unmistakable thread of malaise meandered through the melodies, where younger artists seemed somewhat depressed about the state of affairs we're in. It might not be proactively deliberate, but artists take inspiration from surroundings, and I'd say that sense of malaise has blanketed many of us, artists or not.

For many people there is no question about the life they'll live, the path was set out for us as a middle-class millennial. You'd be familiar with the general expectations of milestones along the journey:

Nuclear family (hopefully no trauma)
Go to university.
Maybe go to London to work a bit.
Find someone to marry.
Get a 'good' 9-5 job.
Have kids.
Buy a house.

Get yourself a bigger car to fit all your kids in.

Revolve your life around your kids, their activities, and school.

Give up dreams about individual travel or art or anything you really wanted to do until you've built a stable life for your family.

Have friendships drop off and be replaced with school social functions.

Keep working 'good jobs' because of the rising interest rates.

Look forward to long service leave.

Keep working.

Look forward to the kids leaving home.

Keep working.

Look forward to retiring.

Retire.

Get sick.

Die.

Of course, I'm being very facetious, but you can pick that there are many elements of this middle-class life journey that we share in common. It's quite easy to float along in this river because that's what we're taught is how we should be. It's a culture, a flow, a mainstream. We might find it comforting to be part of the mainstream. Or maybe we don't even realise we're in it.

It's normal! It's OK! Most people do a version of this. The western world was built for this path. This path was built for us. The society we created geared everything towards being a cog in the capitalist system. It's a standard by which everything and everyone is measured. We all just make the best of it. It's not necessarily 'good' or 'bad'. It sort of just…is.

What is disconcerting though, is that the people who don't want to swim in this stream, or don't measure up to the standard somehow, are often on the outer and perceived negatively. Various groups of people for various reasons are unable to participate in these prescribed activities. Which makes sense, seeing as all humans are different. But there are vilifying news headlines about women who choose not to have children and the unemployed are obviously just bludgers… *eyeroll* …and God forbid if you're a renter or have a disability.

What sometimes comes with this mainstream is a harsh judgmental 'my way or the highway' attitude. What comes with this mainstream is a narrow way of thinking about humans. What it doesn't come with is space for trauma and its generational impacts. What it doesn't come with is the necessary level of empathy to understand nuance. What doesn't come with the mainstream is a leave pass. There is limited permission to be different.

PART 3 - LIFE

Objectively observe how much of this you'd like to participate in. Do you subscribe to the well-worn path, the mainstream ideas, or do you long for some disruption, some other way to do things?

If you're a rebel, an outlier, or you've just had a non-conventional life, you'll be familiar with that nagging feeling that there is something else. Spoiler alert, the antidote is in you. We've already been talking about it. Seeking to understand yourself better, building connections, and embracing that curiosity to see where it might lead.

The antidote is the little anarchies you do every day.

I was at a party in a country hall, finishing up in the outdoor long drop bathroom, washing my hands, and minding my own business as I ventured back out into the dark. I turned the corner and was met with a frightening yelp from a stranger who had been hiding behind the concrete wall. I absolutely crapped myself, gasping audibly and literally jumping. We both started to laugh, she apologised, but I hugged her. It was the best thing that had happened to me in so long. Not many adults go around jump-scaring strangers - for good reason - but this was exactly what I needed. A little anarchy.

163

We are living in a GDP, wealth-centered economic system, that believes our purpose in life is work. We are cogs in a machine, mostly serving the 1% and their endeavours. Their wealth has mostly been built by the exploitation of natural resources and humans. This is not a human-centered system that looks after the planet and people. Sure, there are micro-cultures and alternative paths, but the pervasive system of colonised capitalism dominates. We see it all around us, as more giant corporates open their chain stores in place of small businesses, the thousands of advertisements we see every day, and the cheap K-Mart items we all love to buy, this system has pillaged the world to make a few people wealthier. There has to be other ways.

The foundations of psychology and medicine created a blueprint of what humans are like. What an amazing achievement, we know so much more and can save lives better than we ever have been able to in history. But we are starting to realise that this blueprint was based mostly on white males. Have you read *Invisible Women* by Caroline Criado Perez? Any deviation from this control group has generally been labelled a 'condition'. But in fact, human brains and bodies are extremely diverse, and if we understood and accepted this diversity into our systems, gave more to exploring and researching the different types of people that make up our species, we would have better human outcomes for health and wellness. Possibly even a more unified and positive world, filled with innovative progress and compassion.

We turned away from creativity and connection in favour of individualism and the pursuit of wealth. We used to dance freely, make art and craft, eat food together, and care for our neighbours. But now, these moments have to be stolen, and come few and far between. If it can't be a side hustle, we deem it as unimportant. It's a low priority to dance for the hell of it. Who has time for drawing? Weaving? There is work, and kids, and dinner and laundry, and more work after that.

The system is designed to make us want. Our wanting makes us work. Maybe in jobs we don't care that much about, or long hours in things we do, stressing our bodies, disconnecting us from those we love. And we don't identify that we need less work, and more time with our people, doing things we like. The advertisers get in first with a solution to the emptiness we are experiencing. Makeup or clothes will help you find love, a new TV or car will bring you closer to your family, and this energy drink will give you all the sustenance you need to get through your 12-hour shift! The system created problems and sells us the solutions.

The truth is, we have to work hard to preserve our own time, to carve out our own path, to truly connect to people. Many things will work against this, forcing us to live disconnected from ourselves, and others. Purposefully opening up ourselves to serendipity, to meeting people, being friendly and welcoming can be challenging. But worth it.

Because really, everything we participate in, is all just made-up stuff. The systems? Made up. The law? Made up. Social etiquette? Made up, but I guess it is necessary and inevitable. What distinguishes us from other mammals is our extensive language and ability to make up stories.

If everything is made up, does that mean I can also make up my own story and the way I do things? I'd like to think so, but it's difficult. I've seen people who try to buck the system, and ironically, it doesn't really work unless you have a lot of money. And where would the money come from?

Education prepares us for this capitalist system. Gets us ready for jobs in an office, service or factory. There isn't much onus on people to discover more about who they are, how to handle life situations, and explore their full potential in multiple areas. Although what is now on offer for kids in schools is far progressed from my time at school in the 80s and 90s. But what about the artists? The neurodivergent? The outliers? What about those who don't fit the working model? What about how everything must have a commercial purpose, we must be productive and consuming, or we are worthless!?

Ooh wait, that knock at the door is probably my online shopping order.

There is a path we all get put on, but some of us just don't fit it. We must make space and support people to find their own way of contributing to society. I advocate for creativity and connection as antidotes to the pressures of conformity and consumerism! We can create our own little anarchies.

## ACTIVITY - Little Anarchies

*OK, Jade, you've pointed out all these challenges we have in "system", but what are we supposed to do about that?*

*Great question. I honestly don't know that things can change this late in the game, so many people benefit from the way things are, from the progress we have made. Many people don't see that there even is a problem. Maybe there isn't a problem. But whatever perspective you come from, there's something fun we can do to shake things up with kindness, the way we spend our time, and where we put our money. I see this as an opportunity for little anarchies.*

*I love those stories where someone pays for the coffee order of the person behind them or surprises people with other acts of kindness. Not those people who do it on camera for TikTok views, but just quiet little gestures that make someone's day better. Gosh, even smiling seems like an act of rebellion these days. I often smile at strangers but don't receive the love back. But I won't stop. We have to keep doing these things to bring a counter vibe to the world!*

*Other things that can be done in your own way, every day that reconnect us with humanity and the world.*

- *Buy someone coffee or lunch.*
- *Volunteer your time to a cause you love.*
- *Make art and share it.*
- *Buy Oxfam goats for Christmas instead of more stuff no one needs.*
- *Buy gifts from local businesses.*
- *Go through and give 5-star Google reviews to all your friends' businesses (use some of your doom-scrolling time to do this!)*
- *Check in with the neighbours. Even if you've lived there for 5 years and never spoken.*
- *Leave a nice note or a small piece of art in a library book.*
- *Dance with your kids.*
- *Go to the shop in your pajamas.*
- *Support the small businesses, the artists, the musicians, the makers, the people going out on their own to try and make a living, throw your love and money at them!*

I want to hear about your #littleanarchies please send me stories.

# 22

## *Looking at Social Constructs*

> *"Some'll win, some will lose*
> *Some are born to sing the blues"*
>
> —**Journey**

Culture, social constructs, and power touch every facet of our lives, shaping who we are and how we navigate this complex world. The 'fabric of society' is a collection of ideas and rules woven together as a new set of clothes for the emperor. Clothes that we all put on and take for granted as our uniform. It's everything that makes up our lives - laws and rules, work and business, gender

and identity, economy, education, culture, social class, health and wellbeing, crime and justice, race, ethnicity, national identity... and more. Some kind if concept gets implemented by someone with power, and if people accept and agree to go along with it, it becomes normal reality.

Looking at social constructs is just about observing what is and asking questions about it. The main question I often have is - WHO MADE THESE RULES? Trace it back, have a look, and discover a realisation. I find that's all I can do - I have ideas about what could work better for humanity, but it's not likely I'll make it to parliament, so I'll just hang out in my armchair and keep asking questions. Aiming to adjust my life to better align with my values as I gain more understanding.

This could be a whole book, but all I want to communicate here is that it's important to think about the idea that there is a mainstream way, a standard that is set. We get caught in the standard river because it's the easiest way to flow, but perhaps it's good to take a bigger picture view of how these societal pillars are impacting human outcomes. Maybe there might be alternative ways to think about them. For example, in privileged nations, there is a growing movement seeking alternative methods of education to the regular government-mandated and designed education system. It's viewed by some as archaic, overly bureaucratic, and non-inclusive. But that's a big-picture view - there are incredible teachers dedicated to supporting our kids every single day. But they're burning out at rapid rates...was it all designed as a babysitting service so parents could go to work? Is the curriculum outdated and irrelevant? Is it just another part of the cookie cutter system? Do we start 'indoctrinating' kids too young? Is the list of ever-growing regulatory obligations weighing far too heavily on underfunded institutions? I do not have the answers, but I can understand how people have questions!

Another classic example of social construct in the gender space is a conversation I had with a friend about her husband's transition from living with his parents to moving in with her. She described how his mother had always shouldered the burden of domestic responsibilities, effectively shielding him from the challenges of running a household. As a result, he never learned to juggle multiple external priorities, and everything just magically happened. No need to contemplate how the sheets get clean unless someone directly teaches you, right?

This scenario illustrates a crucial point about culture and social conditioning. Our upbringing and environment contribute significantly to our perception of the world. If you haven't been taught to consider certain aspects of life or if your brain isn't wired to question the status quo, you may simply accept things as they are. My friend faced a twofold challenge. Not only did she have to manage all the household work, but she also had to gently re-train a grown man on what it meant to be in a true partnership. It's a situation that speaks volumes about gender roles and expectations not just in domestic partnerships but broadly in our culture.

Women have fought for their place in the workforce, challenging traditional roles, and seeking equal opportunities. However, the shift toward more inclusive employment opportunities didn't exactly lead to a change in domestic roles. Instead, it added another layer of expectation. Many women are expected to work, care for children, maintain the house, and look after aging parents, all the while, not getting fat, being pretty, and dressing well. It's an overwhelming balancing act, and it's indicative of the deeply embedded power structures that still rule in our social system.

These disparities give rise to diverse opinions and narratives. For example, the old 'pull yourself up by your bootstraps' is a common idea from some people that the only thing stopping a person in poverty from being rich is a little bit of hard work. Others contend that systemic disadvantages require significant government intervention and wealth redistribution. What a battle this is. Hell, even poor people advocate for low tax rates for billionaires, because one day, they too might just become rich.

There isn't anything wrong with differences in thinking, that's healthy and interesting! It's what we do when confronted with contrasting ideas that matters. In the age of the internet, everyone can tell their own story, and there is no moderation in the wild west of the web. We're exposed to a barrage of information and opinions some credible, some not. Algorithms feed us, and some dive right into the extremism rabbit hole. This informational chaos contributes to division. The more divided we become, the more we fear the "other," and the more we retreat into our own bubbles.

We seek out safety in our echo chambers, where our values are mirrored back to us. It feels secure, but it's a false sense of security. These bubbles create division, reinforcing our biases and pushing us further away from understanding those with different perspectives.

We might believe we have choices in the content we consume, but we're often spoon-fed stories by major media outlets, social media algorithms, and the broader internet of ads. It's a double-edged sword. We're starting to see the fragility of democracy as people are easily swayed by online information. Yet, we, including myself, spend hours immersed in this digital realm every day.

The emergence of Artificial Intelligence (AI) adds another layer of complexity. Misinformation, deepfakes, and biased algorithms amplify the risk of division and misunderstanding. Further division on important issues means we spend energy fighting about problems rather than actively solving them. This all just adds to the undercurrent of strain that we are experiencing in this modern life.

It's OK to feel overwhelmed about all this. Look at all that's happening around us! We're navigating a world shaped by a challenging history, culture and social constructs, and power dynamics that are deeply ingrained and resistant to change. It shouldn't be a surprise that mental health is declining, and we feel more and more disconnected. Or you might not feel overwhelmed at all, and you're doing fine in your bubble. If you are, I'm jealous.

It comes back to remembering our shared humanity. We're all just trying to make sense of a complex world, each with our own perspectives and experiences. Empathy, critical thinking, and a feast around a fire should fix it!

Is there potential to head toward a more inclusive, equitable, and understanding world? Surely the systems we trust in would have our back!? They'd be inclusive and equitable, easy to navigate, and human-centered...wouldn't they?

## ACTIVITY - Creative Activation

*The world can be a lot. Life can be a lot. I believe that the innate creativity inside us is designed to help us process all of that. One of the most common things that people say to me when I'm teaching creative workshops is "Oh I'm not creative" or "I used to be creative." I say NONSENSE! I think what people mean is "I'm not good enough at creative things to make it a commercial venture" Because we're conditioned to believe that we have to be 'good' at it. Or there's an underlying cultural idea that everything we do has to have some kind of money-making purpose. We do not have to make creativity a side hustle. We can and should be creative for the sake of it. Because it's good for our souls because it helps us understand the world because it supports us in processing life. I believe all humans are creative. We all started out as toddlers communicating by drawing pictures!*

*Somewhere this gets lost, and we take on different beliefs about our abilities or the value of creativity.*

*If you approach creativity with zero expectations on yourself, an open and mindful heart, the potential benefits of creativity are:*

- *Time to yourself or social connection - whichever way you choose to engage. Do it yourself or take some classes!*
- *Reducing stress and improving mood – self-expression and processing life events.*
- *Enhanced problem-solving and cognition - using a different part of your brain.*
- *Focus and concentration - forgetting all the worries of the day and giving attention to the task.*
- *Processing emotions.*

*I've already talked about some activities you can do to get creative in the process of understanding yourself, but here are a few more suggestions for incorporating creativity into your life mindfully and purposefully so that you can feel these benefits.*

- *Cook something new, follow the recipe or chuck it in the bin and just make something up! I love getting inspiration from videos on social media and then winging it to see what I can come up with.*
- *Get a sketchbook and pen, carry it around with you and when you get a chance, do some drawing, doodling, or writing. This is a super easy way to start incorporating some 'creative brain' action in your life. Take 10 minutes when you go get your morning coffee, pull it out when you're waiting for an appointment, and quick sketch on the train - there is space for this when you look for it.*

- *Do some non-work related creative writing - it's easy to find prompts on the internet for story-telling, or you could journal your thoughts and feelings. If that's too unstructured, try writing a morning intention and an evening gratitude.*
- *Gardening is an art AND a science, and it's so good to get your hands in the soil. Yes, it's totally creative. You're developing an environment for something to grow in, how wonderful!*
- *Another super simple one, is to get into some of your favourite music. Put it on in the morning, or while you're throwing together that dinner. Reminisce, have a dance, and lift the mood of your space.*

# 23

## Challenging Systems and the Bureaucracy

*"Well we don't need no one to tell us what to do
Oh yes we're on our own
And there's nothing you can do"*

—The Living End

Let's look for a moment at these systems that we trust in and rely on, or rather, must endure on any given day of existence. There are a few categories that make up the spiderweb of structures we are entangled in:

- **Society:** Housing, Economy, Healthcare, Education, Politics, Government
- **Social:** Family, Friends, Community
- **Culture:** Religion, Ethics, Belief Structures
- **Employment:** Work, Banks, Business
- **Technology:** Personal Devices, Entertainment, Work related

There are just so many touch points to manage, and complex pathways to navigate on any regular day, let alone if we're dealing with something more difficult. When we go through the big hard stuff, there is always a couple of sides to it. There's the intense emotional part and then usually there's these bureaucratic, difficult processes to go through.

The key to dealing with what feels like total garbage is to manage expectations around what's to come. This could also be a whole book, but having been through several of these major events, I can tell you that there is a lot of paperwork and relationship management involved. Often, much of it seems unnecessary and elongates the process. Processes are usually in place to help. Even if it doesn't feel like it. We live in a very complicated world these days, which also makes things longer and harder. There are lots of decisions to make, and paper chains to navigate.

All these systems, structures, foundations, and institutional systems, while doing their best to serve, cause stress. Over time, processes get added to rather than simplified, creating layers of fuckery that we must deal with while we are in the pits of despair.

These aspects of society are so bureaucratic and arduous, often archaic and made of patchwork processes. Rarely are they are functioning as a smooth, logical journey with a clearly defined outcome and simple steps to get there.

These processes that need to be adhered to haven't necessarily been designed with humans in mind. They're often centred around the goals of the organisation, instead of the user's experience. We can feel so overwhelmed and despondent dealing with these impersonal systems.

One example is around dealing with a mysterious, rare, yet non-life-threatening condition (the Chiari Malformation thing). When you're unwell, you need health care. As adequate and helpful as the system is in Australia, it's very challenging to navigate and feel like you're winning. I personally was pretty traumatized by my experiences. It took over 6 years to get the medical procedure I needed, hundreds of appointments, misunderstandings, failed attempts at other solutions, and bureaucratic processes.

When I told someone that I was traumatized, I got the same response as many doctors had given me; disbelief and "But the public system is great." It really is, especially compared to many systems in the world, and I am grateful to have had this major surgery at no financial cost. So, I acknowledge my privilege, but it still wasn't particularly easy for me, and I know that others have similar challenges. Medicine has become quite amazing at saving lives and limbs in common situations, and the efforts of incredibly dedicated healthcare professionals never cease to amaze me. But there is a puzzle in long-term chronic conditions with overlapping symptoms that are hard to identify the cause of. Maybe if I'd had a common and easy condition to manage, things would have been different.

I needed to learn the language of healthcare professionals to tick the right boxes to get the right help. I needed to learn to push through my trauma and fear and advocate for myself. Repeatedly. I needed to push through the dismissive attitudes I often encountered and convince people that what I was experiencing was not OK and I needed more help from them.

These same types of challenges arise everywhere, every week in every life challenge. Forms, processes, fees, phone calls, don't even get me started on logins and passwords!

So then, as you, and many people around you deal with these complex webs, it's likely there are some that are a bit stressed, frustrated, and confused. Another reason why it's so important to be compassionate. If someone shares with you that they have a chronic health condition, just know that they've probably been through a lot of literal and figurative pain, endless appointments and frustrating processes. If that person is you, god speed.

Here are a few tips on how I personally deal with this stuff.

1. Scream into the void every time a new challenge arises.
2. Fish around in my skull for a sense of logic.
3. Once said logic is found, formulate a plan on how to tackle the process.
4. Gird my loins, because the only way through is to fight.

Advocating for myself has been the single hardest, but most effective way to get things done in shitty situations. It is very unfortunate that we must be stronger than usual in our hardest times, but this is how it is. It's best to manage expectations, pick a good time to tackle the work required, call in a friend if you need to, and feel proud once you're through it.

Let's take a medical process as an example. You start off with some symptoms, and sometimes it's an easy fix. Great! But if it's something a bit more mysterious or chronic, it's like taking on a whole project.

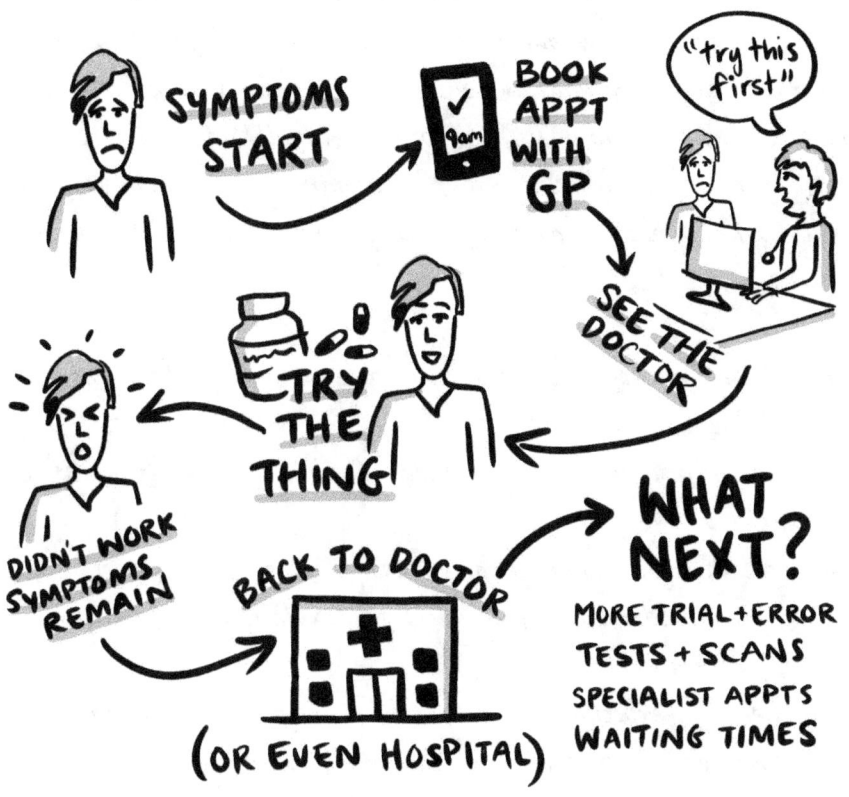

It could be helpful to take some time to preempt what might happen, research the process you're about to embark on, and plan for time and energy around it. I know I did NOT do this, and got extremely overwhelmed over and over again, because my expectations were not aligned with reality of how long things take. Tackling any bureaucratic system requires a healthy dose of patience, which will certainly be tested!

## ACTIVITY - Map Out the Process

*Facing the challenge of any of these processes can be daunting. For some people, they love it! If you are like me, and you don't really get a buzz from forms and processes, writing, drawing, mapping out the process ahead of you can help a lot. Manage expectations, and act as a guide for your journey. A more visual map will act as a step by step to-do list, and you can see it all laid out. It will help you manage expectations and achieve your life admin with less stress. I sometimes even do this just to map out a day's activities, so I know what to expect and have my anxiety reduced.*

- *Map out the steps that it takes to get to a diagnosis and treatment for illness.*
- *Do some internet research on relevant websites for whatever task you have to do*
- *Find an expert - someone you know or find an online support group and ask loads of questions. People explaining the process will help immensely.*
- *There is no expectation to create a masterpiece, just scribbling or doodling it will provide some relief for the mind and vision for what's to come.*

# 24

*Comparing, Contrasting, Critically thinking*

*"I'm sad, but I'm laughing
I'm brave, but I'm chicken shit
I'm sick, but I'm pretty, baby"*

—Alanis Morrisette

Remember in university when we were asked to 'compare and contrast' a particular topic to demonstrate understanding? Comparing to see what's similar, and contrasting to see what is different.

Contrast is my favourite design principle.

I love seeing, or putting things together, that are unexpected, but somehow each provides a contrast to the other, to make each other more apparent. But the important thing to note is that opposing things can co-exist.

I love wearing combat boots with feminine tulle. Or sparkly sneakers with a corporate dress.

I love black and white.

I love having The Beatles on the same playlist as metal songs.

There is always dark and light. In everything. It's a universal principle.

Yin and yang. Good and evil. Day and night. Hot and cold.

There can't be light without darkness, and vice versa. They both exist to make each other more apparent.

It's this critical thinking that will help understand the relationship between things in life, because everything is connected in some way, and everything is different in some way. But all the opposites are there for us to experience.

In life, in relationships, this principle helps you see clearer. It's important to know where you are the same and where you are different to people in your world. We forget that people shouldn't just be like us. What a boring fucking world if we were all the same.

The bright sunshine wouldn't be so lovely if we didn't have the moody night.

If I didn't have 17 jerk idiot boyfriends, how would I know about healthy and magnificent love?

If I didn't have my house flooded, how would I know true community spirit?

If I didn't binge drink and have terrible hangovers, how would I know about how good it is to feel fresh on a Sunday morning?

I know it's a bit of a cliche, but it's what I've known to help my life.

Knowing the similarities and differences between people, culture, your own views, and others, can help you make decisions. If you approach this with curiosity, you it can help you have empathy, adapt your communication and behaviour, be accommodating to others, and come to acceptance about how things are. You may discover interesting threads of contrasting ideas to follow and have an opportunity to connect on ideas that are similar. This helps you decide what your own alignment is, what your interests and values are.

Comparing and contrasting to ourselves is probably the most valuable application of this principle if we want to change something in life. We should spend less time comparing our own work to the achievements of others, and more time comparing our yesterday self to our current self.

People are looking for balance, in the way of weighting things equally. 'Balancing' work, giving equal amounts of time to all our priorities, but I think balance is different.

Balance in the world is about this principle of contrast.

It's about dark and light.

Yin and yang.

Positive and negative.

Yes and no.

Birth and death.

Masculine and feminine. (If you want to identify with these. Maybe not identifying with either is the perfect point of balance, and we could all learn some things from non-binary crew.)

They all exist together. We all exist together. Who the hell knows why, but we do.

Yes, we have to work at balance, but it's not about the practicality of juggling the demands of day-to-day life, it's about intangible, immeasurable feelings about your life. It's about embracing the dark with the light, seeing the cycles, seeking out what's needed to bring some equilibrium to our perspective.

Balance is about the right measures of yin and yang in your soul. Woo woo, I know. But hear me out.

OK, so, if life seems difficult, like there is more dark than light, sometimes changing a practical element isn't always possible. As much as I dream about running away from all this adulting, unfortunately we can't escape the responsibilities and limitations in our lives. We must accept them and seek to find more light in the seemingly perpetual darkness. This is the work to do.

The opposite is true too.

If we are coasting along, with 100% 'light filled' life, easy and safe, there probably isn't enough grit, and we might be a bit stagnant. I'm not saying go and seek out the dark prince, unless that's your thing, but perhaps engage with some things that will challenge you. Start a new thing either practically, or just within yourself. Get uncomfortable.

PART 3 - LIFE

That happy light you were chasing may just start to dim on its own anyway. Sandpaper will always come along to rough up your smooth sailing existence. Have you noticed that? It's impossible to exist without the contrast of opposing things. It's the cycle of life.

Plants grow with the right amount of dark and light. Their roots remain in the dark, while leaves catch the sun.

Whales live in the dark depths of the ocean, but they must come up for sun and air at times.

There are so many examples of how this principle exists in nature and believe it or not - you might have forgotten, like I do sometimes - we are part of nature. We are part of these universal principles.

My passionate drive is to understand systems, cultures, human behavior, and it means that I continually see problems and come up with solutions. But what I've realised, is that many of these problems we fight to solve will never be solved. The yin and the yang ensure a balance of dark and light. We strive for entirety of light, but it wouldn't be light without the contrast of dark. For thousands of years humanity has sought to evolve into enlightenment but collectively we seemed to have missed the memo and at times, delved too darkly.

Sometimes, where one problem is solved, another is created. Where someone comes out of poverty, some other resource is diminished. When one war finishes, another one begins. We just haven't seemed to be able to get it right. Perhaps true evolution is this realisation that light and dark must co-exist in harmony. We must endure suffering to enjoy the good things of life. We have to accept the shadow to appreciate the sunshine. Embracing differences, seeking balance, and acknowledging the perpetual interplay of light and dark in our lives - I don't know why, but that just seems to be how we move through.

## ACTIVITY – Attitude Journal

*If we're geared towards thinking in a dark space, this can be really helpful to start training the brain to see what's light. And if we don't ever consider the downsides for others, we can't enjoy the fullest appreciation for our own good times.*

*Sure, there's the old gratitude journal, but what about the Attitude Journal? We are so uncomfortable about 'negative emotions' in our culture. We love to shove them under the carpet. Until there's so many under there that you trip over and fall on your face. We have to accept that as a human, you have a wide range of feelings, and that is a beautiful thing!*

*You could begin a practice of deliberately writing about what you feel is going well, AND not so well in life. Write a pros and cons list for the day. What emotions did you feel about certain events? Furious about what happened? Great! It means you're feeling something.*

I don't believe it's 'negative' to examine what situations make us feel angry, sad, frustrated or down. It gives us an opportunity to feel the fullness of all our human emotions. We don't have to stay in those places, but we also shouldn't shove those feelings down and ignore what they are telling us. Feel that contrast in life and get more comfortable with your uncomfortable feelings.

# MY PROS AND CONS DIARY

# 25

## *Feeling the Disproportionate BS*

*"Everything, everything, everything is awful"*

—The Decemberists

As you might have seen, I do love to tell a good story about the calamities of existence. I feel like I'm often having shit go 'wrong'. This chapter is for when you're feeling shitty, in a depressive episode, and just need to relate to someone. Life is a flip flop between hot and cold, but just like the week has 7 days, it's all a bit lopsided. There is that contrast of dark and light, and sometimes it feels totally disproportionate. You're going through some hard stuff. I feel you. In the last few years, I've had a trail of major life challenges, which has brought me to this place of working out how to get through them with my heart and mind:

Marriage break up.
Packed up a creative business and went back to an office job.
Bankruptcy.
Painful Chiari Malformation illness and neurosurgery.
Financial fuck ups to do with insurance, not of my doing.
Lost a job.
Unemployed for 18 months.
Moved house three times - one because of the financial fuck up, one by choice, and another time because my home flooded.
Adenomyosis and Endometriosis diagnosis.
Gynecological surgery.
3 more job changes.
A new creative business.
Kids becoming teenagers. IYKYK.

Yes, yes, it's all about finding the light in the inevitable darkness, but it's OK to let all the stuff be shitty for a while. It's HARD.

In a single day recently, I woke up to a Centrelink debt and they'd cut my payments, then as I got ready to leave for work, suddenly one of kids is sick and needs to stay home from school. Then the realtor does a surprise visit with a property valuer, which is always a good sign for a renting tenant. Then there's something wrong with my kid's laptop and it takes me 2.5 hours and a lot of tears to work it out. Then for some reason, I made the foolish mistake of weighing myself.

You get the drift; you're having days like this too. Shit just goes wrong. Existence seems so hard. I'm often waiting for big positive things to happen, like some kind of balance. But sometimes I'm certain that the 80/20 rule applies to the suffering/happiness ratio.

If our memory bank is filled with more trauma than joy, that's often the  place we operate from. And the more you experience, the more you can lose yourself into the results of trauma. I am definitely not an expert, but I have spent a lot of time living from this place as traumatic experiences have compounded over time. Frustration, burnout, anger, sadness, malaise, unexpected dysregulation, are all things I feel in a big way.

You've heard by now the hours of therapy I've put myself through, read about all these ways we can be kinder and happier and better for ourselves and each other. But life just isn't all roses! Although I'm sure there are some lucky people that just don't get bitten by the bad luck bug and are actually content and optimistic. Wow! I love that journey for you. For lots of people though, there are many reasons to cry yourself to sleep at night. Hopefully not every night, but it's a thing...right?

I've had these super challenging times, and there are a few things working against me in this system and life, but I do feel really lucky.

Lots of cool stuff happens too… I had a really successful art show after my house flooded, the new business is going slowly but well, I started running art workshops, I've written a book! I acknowledge that I have some privilege, I've been able to work hard and get myself into a better position on my own. I have a lovely apartment I'm renting right now, I have two amazing teen girls, who challenge me, but I absolutely adore and want the best for. I have some incredible friends who accept me and love me and cheer me on. I have a partner who is loving, kind and genuinely wants to see me succeed. Brisbane is a good city. It might not have the pizazz of Melbourne or the vibe of NYC, but it's sunny, moving forward, and is a level of manageable busy. It's also in the middle of incredibly beautiful natural locations. Beaches, rivers, rainforest…

A truck comes to take my rubbish away. I have clean water to drink. My plants get better drinking water than millions of people in this world.

I have a really amazing collection of health professionals, even though it costs me, they help me so much. My kids have access to really good public schools.

I am so often dwelling on what I believe to be lacking, missing, haven't achieved, not good enough in. When we spend too long in that place we can only handle so much before the compounding effects of traumatic experiences start to chip away at our souls, and the existential dread tugs on your torso. Perpetual disappointments, daily depression, even utter pain as you open your eyes in the morning…I've been there too. Probably just last week.

But…I can paint, write, spend time with friends, go on holidays, enjoy delicious food and drinks. Yes. It's getting more expensive and harder, and it does feel like all this could very easily slip away with another illness or job change or forced move. But right now, I'm looking for these beautiful treats.

What inkling of light can you find? There's always something, no matter how insignificant it might seem. Maybe it's the smile from a stranger, or a cute puppy, or you might need to go buy yourself something delicious or take a walk outside.

Also, what about music! How good is music! And flowers! How lovely are they?!

I constantly try to optimise and problem solve to improve the human experience, but I know hard times will always keep coming.

So despite finding the joy, sometimes things go a bit awry. I know, I can slip into a raincloud of anxiety so easily. But I try to turn it into a funny story, or find that pin prick of light. It helps me deal with it. This somewhat cheerfully cynical view has assisted me to look objectively at the ridiculousness of the world we live in and find the humour in the haystack of horrors. We absolutely cannot take this shit seriously. As I've said, I call myself an optimistic nihilist. I want things to better in the world, but I know that they probably can't be. I too want more light than dark, but it's unlikely to recalibrate. So, I'm left to laugh at the absurdity of this existence.

Life is made of big challenges and small joys.

What I'm here to say, is that tomorrow might be better. Or the next hour. Or even the next minute, if you can find it within you to notice something small. A small joy. (I've heard this being called a 'glimmer' - the opposite of a 'trigger').

You'll see the clouds and think they're pretty (but then your car won't start), or you'll have a nice text message from a friend, (but then miss the bus), you'll have a lovely lunch (and then get some hard financial news), maybe by then lose your shit and cry. This is the beauty of life. The trick is to try to minimise its impact on you.

It's just about slowing down, feeling the feeling, taking that breath, and then moving forward. What's the next thing to do?

It's about trying to have a good minute. And then a good hour. Then a good day is made up of good hours. And a year is made up of good days... but really, it's made up of good minutes. So, try to have a good minute in between the challenging ones.

I have coached myself into seeing the beauty in everyday things, because I know there is a lot of joy to be found. I actively appreciate moments like butterflies and sunshine, my kids when they aren't scratching each other's eyes out, and funny memes.

When I can get a breath, I really do work on bringing myself into the present, doing the old....five things I can see, four things I can hear, three stinky things in the rubbish bin, two sharp things I could throw across the room etcetera, etcetera.

I mean, as beautiful as a butterfly is on a sunshiny day, I feel like it would take 4,392 of them to make up for one phone call to a telephone company. The proportions sometimes just seem all wrong.

But I come back to the notion that we are destined for this contrast – light and dark, yin and yang, good and evil, hard and easy. If you fail to see that this is how things operate, it makes it difficult to find the good, and I don't know that you can understand the world. It's this thing I have about the dark and the light again. I don't think it's a 50/50 scenario. They both have to exist in tandem, but the proportions of what you see and experience, might very well just be up to you.

## ACTIVITY – Yin and Yang

*What examples of yin and yang, dark and light, opposing forces have you observed, in nature, in life? What instances of light are there in the presence of darkness? What instances of darkness are there in the presence of light?*

# 26

## *The Meaning Matrix*

*"Is there life on mars?"*

—David Bowie

So, what do we make of all this? Examining life, looking at the bigger picture, asking deep questions, accepting the dark with the light - maybe you want to close the book at this point and go and make a drink. I don't blame you. But I do have one more idea to share.

It is a natural human state to search for meaning. We can see that the world is complex, challenging, and far from perfect. But what criteria do we use when we're trying to figure out what life is really about for us as individuals. What parts of all that do we gravitate towards?

It's pretty absurd, I don't know that there are really any solid criteria for purpose, I've seen a news article about a woman getting married to a fencepost, so the search for meaning can go far and wide. However, this is my idea.

I've worked out a way to organise the foundational elements of existence into loosely held categories. I believe that there are four quadrants when we look for meaning, something to put hope into and our energy towards. It's what we end up caring about and living for.

We all sit somewhere in this matrix as a predominant place that we find meaning for life. Of course, you might identify with a couple, or all of these in different ways. It's a way to think about the context that we live in in this modern world, various things that we believe in as humans, and how we might purposefully contribute to the betterment of existence.

Religion is an interesting aspect, as it is human made, but also intangible. Sometimes religion is more about the rules, sometimes it's more about the spiritual aspect. This is not a perfect, researched academic output, it's an observation and an idea about how we could think about how the world works and where folks find solace.

The 'meaning of life' is a deeply personal exploration, unique to every human. Personally, I find meaning in the little things, like, chocolate in the afternoon and 6 glasses of wine on a Friday. But really, through our lives, we are likely to explore many aspects of this model, and either land somewhere we feel comfortable, or continue to be curious about all four quadrants. They are not mutually exclusive. You might love Jesus and believe in the power of AI to change humanity for the better. You might believe in tarot card readings from a psychic, and also work as a CEO for a big company. We are more than one thing, and we don't really fit into boxes.

Our identity, the way we relate to others and how we deal with life can be impacted by all these concepts or only some of them. Part of this is about exploring your own place, your beliefs and what influences your responses to challenges and life events. But wherever you sit, this is just a reminder to look beyond the day-to-day and see that beyond our selves, and our relationships, there are many things that can influence our lives.

# Jade's Meaning Matrix:

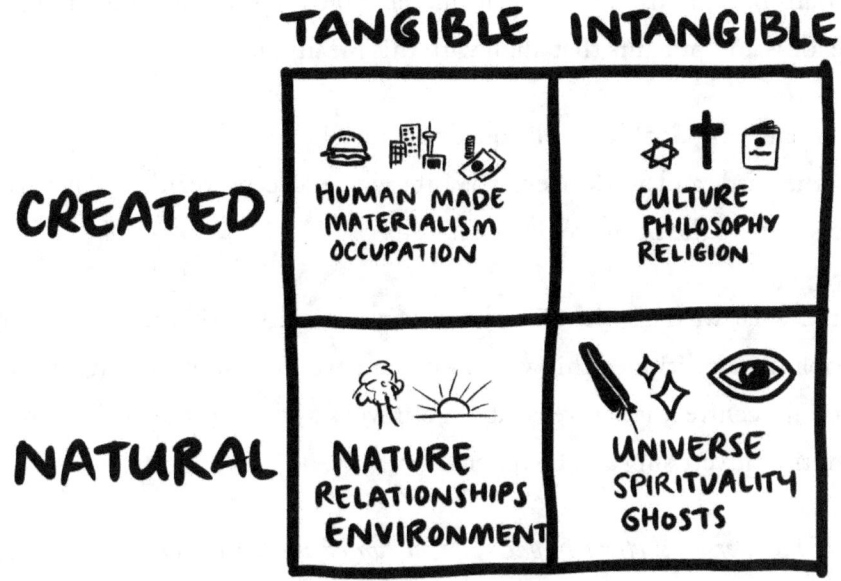

## CREATED/TANGIBLE

**Quadrant 1: Human Made Existence**

Here in this first quadrant, it's all about the tangible stuff we can touch and the world we've created as humans. Human made and not particularly open to the unknown. Life is 100% what you make, and you 100% die at the end.

This is the perspective that emphasises the tangible and human-made aspects of life as the primary sources of meaning. Material wealth, achievements, and societal success

are some of the things that would sit here. The systems, processes, bureaucracy that we contend with might come easier to someone in this zone. Humanism, materialism, capitalism, individualism, technology, physical comfort might all be ideas and pursuits that align with this meaning.

Individuals who dabble in this quadrant may believe that existence is just about the hustle and bustle of everyday life, where success, wealth, and material possessions are the ultimate purpose.

Most of what we deal with on a day-to-day basis sits in this realm, so we're probably all conditioned this way to a certain extent. Ambition and achievements take centre stage as we go about our work and life, influenced strongly by politics, advertising and commercial culture.

BELIEFS: *Personal effort impacts life outcomes, master of your own destiny, humans' rule, hustle, tech, ambition, consumerism, personal comfort.*

POTENTIAL PURPOSE LED ACTION: *Mentoring, coaching, supporting business or nonprofit ventures, financial counseling, housing, food, medicine, tech advancements.*

# CREATED/INTANGIBLE

### Quadrant 2: Theoretical and Metaphysical

This part is all about intangible aspects of human existence, such as the pursuit of knowledge, personal growth, and self-discovery. Human

thoughts and ideas form social structures, politics, culture, values, religions, and philosophies, offering the opportunity for deep thinking about purpose and understanding. It's where we explore human potential and question the very essence of existence itself, both as individuals and collectively. Part of religion sits here, with the development of creed and doctrine, where people find life guidance and their own meaning and truth.

Curiosity about how the mind works, sociological rules, philosophy, culture, ethics as we live our lives on this earth is what occupies this space. This quadrant always leads to the ultimate existential question... why?

It's about creating narratives, understanding our values, and searching for a sense of belonging and significance in the important yet somewhat intangible aspects of being a human. How we relate to ourselves, one another, and broader ideas is a central theme of philosophy, sociology and religion. There is the important element of love, connection and relationship here in this quadrant.

*BELIEFS: Structures impact life outcomes, humanism, relationship, ethical living, emotional life, personality tests, philosophy and introspection, following traditions and philosophies that many humans before us have followed, created to make sense of existence.*

*POTENTIAL PURPOSE LED ACTION: Religious volunteering/organisations, mentoring, homelessness prevention, work against violence, suicide prevention, community building, health care, education, mentoring.*

# NATURAL/TANGIBLE

**Quadrant 3: Biological and Evolutionary**

Here, in this third quadrant, we're getting back to our roots, the raw, tangible aspects of life. It aligns with a perspective rooted in the natural world, science, biological and  evolutionary principles. The meaning of life is seen to be connected to the fundamental drive for survival, reproduction, and the continuation of the species on this planet. Perhaps also looking to the preservation of the ecosystem to ensure the survival of future generations.

Can life's purpose truly be reduced to just surviving and ensuring the survival of our species? Or is there something more profound, something that transcends our biological makeup?

Connection to proven theories of science, evidence, and an underlying sense that we are just another animal occupying the earth are the ideas for this quadrant. We live, we connect to others, we die, there isn't anything too significant other than we live by our biological survival instincts and perhaps have the view that we are to be good stewards of the earth we live on.

*BELIEFS: Nature, earth, science, space, survival, our connection to nature, we are another animal on the earth, a speck in the universe, we live, we die, science has proven, we see the value in what exists in this realm and seek to protect it.*

*POTENTIAL PURPOSE LED ACTION: Environmental action, animal protection, food equality, climate change industry, scientific discovery, education.*

# NATURAL/INTANGIBLE

**Quadrant 4: Spiritual and Transcendental**

Quadrant 4 explores the intangible mystical aspects of life. From a spiritual and transcendent perspective, meaning is often sought through meditation, mindfulness, 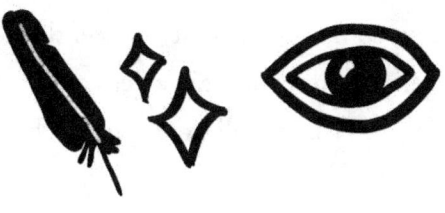 and spiritual practices. The other half of religion and spiritual belief systems fall into this quadrant, with a belief in higher power that keeps us accountable to our creed. This zone might suggest that the ultimate purpose of life is to seek transcendence, inner peace, or a connection with a cosmic consciousness.

It's the spiritual journey of connection between our inner selves and the pursuit of peace in something beyond the material and logical world around us. We might look to gurus or psychics, or gifted ones with insight beyond what is right in front of us. We might join a church, we might have been raised with strong spiritual guidance, we might use prayer, meditation, or manifestation as a daily practice. There is potential here for the consideration of life after death, karma, reincarnation…ghosts?!

Is there a higher purpose? Is there a cosmic universal spirit guiding us? Are there greater forces at work, supporting our journey?

*BELIEFS: The universe, spirituality, luck, chance, fate, supernatural forces, superstition, coincidence, predetermined fate, our destiny is not our own choice, other forces are at work, magical and at the whim of external unseen forces.*

*POTENTIAL PURPOSE LED ACTION: Mentoring, coaching, religious work, energetics.*

Even though there are different arenas of making meaning, there must be a collective commonality that transcends them and unites us in some way. Despite differences in beliefs and ideas about what the real meaning of life is, there are things that we all experience as humans. Beyond being born, living, and dying, there are shared elements of human existence that can bring us together if we step back and look beyond these principles of the Meaning Matrix. The complexity and richness of human existence can be shared through these activities, no matter where we make our meaning.

- Communication
- Creative expression – art, music, writing, dancing and story telling
- Emotions and feelings
- Sharing of knowledge and education
- Sharing of responsibilities and problem solving
- Working and obtaining resources
- The need for connection and to be understood
- Food, nourishment and health

These things are universally human experiences, from our most basic survival instincts to our quest for meaning, connection, and understanding. Encompassing both our shared needs and the challenges we encounter in navigating the complexities of life, these elements can be found interwoven across cultures and societies as foundations of existence. We live in this modern world, enjoying so many benefits, but we may have lost the focus on some of these very important elements of humanity along the way.

Whichever corner you find yourself gravitating to, let it spark some ideas. Let this be an opening to consider more about yourself and the world, create more meaning, and live more purposefully towards the things that matter to you.

## ACTIVITY - Your Personal Contribution Statement

*It's another journaling exercise! Don't be like that, just get the pen and paper, OK. This is where you ponder all the things you've thought about throughout the journey of this book and explore where you're at. Working towards a statement about your own personal purpose.*

*What parts of this matrix resonate with you? Why?*
*Do any of the purpose led actions light up your soul?*
*Would you add more or different ones?*

# Contribution Statement

*I value:*

*I believe:*

*I care about:*

*I will:*

# 27

*Embracing Life*

*"Shiny happy people holding hands."*

—R.E.M

Well, here we are, all ready to sing kumbaya and start a 'new year new me' regime! It's been a journey, some challenging parts, and hopefully some lighter, relatable parts. Let's take a look at where we've been...

## WE ARE CONNECTED TO OURSELVES. OR NOT.

Part 1 is all about this, and if I haven't said it enough, I'll summarise again here.

We get so disconnected from ourselves, forgetting, or never understanding who we are. You'll know this by the state of your mental health, how you feel about certain people or activities, or a niggling feeling that something isn't right.

This discontentment is a disconnection from understanding what your PREFERENCES, PRIORITIES and PATTERNS are. You might ignore it for a while, lots of people ignore it their whole lives, finding ways to board up the windows and abandon it altogether. However, the best way to start dealing with all the challenges and triumphs that life brings is to take a look at this and see what you can find out about the essence of you.

Open up your creativity for pathways towards deeper understanding, to activate dormant parts of you, to engage with the world in a fresh way. What resonates as purposeful living for you? What do you care about?

Communicate with yourself more compassionately. Be open to change in yourself. Take responsibility for your life. Redefine your defining moments. This is an antidote to an existential crisis. Or maybe the start of one, but I promise you can get through it.

## HUMANS ARE CONNECTED.

We know that. Or at least if we've made it this far through the book, we should know it by now. What have we learned?

Acceptance of each other.
Acceptance of our emotions.
Relieving one another's suffering.

But we cannot get there unless we are mindfully communicating and deliberately connecting. There is a love within all of us that we can tap into once we drop the facade. It isn't realllly going to be all 'shiny happy people holding hands', but we could try and find that centre of the Venn diagram with other people and have a nicer time.

We talked about vulnerability, and obviously I'm not the first to do so, but I want to reiterate in my own words that understanding yourself, being real and vulnerable and being truly just you, is what connection is built on.

If you feel disconnected, let some of your facade fall down and just be. Be wherever you are. Be with people. Take with you an intention of love, joy, connection, and your experience will improve. Allow your feelings of frustration, overwhelm or even anger to exist, but don't let them overrule in your engagement with those around you.

Entering into the world of another is a remedy for disconnection with them. Empathy, compassion, curiosity... Being present and asking questions, letting go of your expectations on them, and we can hope they would do the same for us. It's hard to do this if we haven't accepted our selves. If you are still floundering around believing you are the only injured one of the herd trying to find solutions to a problem all on your own, it's time to look beyond.

We need each other. We seem more divided and distracted than ever before in human existence, so now is the time to nurture and celebrate relationship. Not just to those in our immediate sphere, but a broader acceptance and active compassion for those you don't know, or even understand. Expand your energy to be connected beyond your bubble in whatever way that looks like for you. For me, it's even just smiling at strangers, even though I get mad when they don't smile back. It's having a little chat to the barista, telling someone they look stylish, trying really hard to make small talk even though I am anxiety ridden and socially awkward. It might be donating to organisations that are supporting a cause you connect with, or volunteering for something you've never done before. There are so many ways to extend your connection with other people.

## WE ARE CONNECTED TO EVERYTHING.

We can't find clarity by only looking at ourselves. Or even those around us. We must look beyond, examining where we are at this point in time. Understand that the bigger picture impacts our personal journey. The systems, culture, social constructs, institutions, the earth all play a part in shaping who we are and how we engage with life. Our unique selves respond differently to different aspects of these threads that make up the fabric of society.

But we have to rise above our political opinions, our ideologies, and find the common ground. The key aspects of humanity that we all share, and the universal truths of how we live.

Purpose is what you create. Making lemonade is just about finding your own meaning in the light and dark of life. Purpose isn't hidden under the couch; it isn't one key task that you must fulfill (although some people seem to have a very clear life mission), it's not a tangible item to discover. Purpose is finding out who you are, how to connect, what you believe in, then taking these things and moving forward to contribute to the world through things that you enjoy. Not to say that a purposeful existence won't have challenges and boring bits. It totally will. But the closer you are to living yours, the more confident you'll be when the lemons start flying. You will find resilience and fulfillment in the alignment you build.

Just remember too, we must laugh. After all, we're just little specks on a blue dot, floating around in an unfathomable infinity, so nothing can be taken too seriously.

Good luck and best wishes with making YOUR lemonade. Let me know how it goes.

x Jade

# Acknowledgements

Writing a book is a wild adventure to embark on. It's so much more than just words on a page. It's heart, soul, sweat and tears! There are some people I want to say particular thanks to, and many more who have supported me on the journey.

**Madeline and Scarlett** – my gorgeous daughters, you keep me going in this crazy world. I love you more than I can ever explain, and I wish an incredible, fulfilling, adventurous and generous life for you.

**Dan** - Thank you for your unwavering love and support, for listening to me patiently as I go around in circles with all my wild projects, and for believing in me endlessly.

**Tim** – I appreciate you so much and couldn't ask for a better co-parenting scenario. We're doing alright.

**Leanne** –You asked me if you could read my first very raw draft, which was the catalyst for getting this project done in 2023. You are such a rad friend, and I appreciate your advice, encouragement and very existence, just being who you are and doing what you do.

Everyone who read this early and gave me testimonials, advice and support. YOU ARE THE BEST.

**Kelly and the Expert Author Community** – Thank you so much for your support, invaluable guidance, and resources that you have developed to support people on the writing ride. (Highly recommend joining this for anyone who wants to write a book.)

**Meg** – for your early help with editing, it was great timing to be able to share this with you and have your encouragement.

**Stef** – my Manifesto Mate for your encouragement and support.

To all my friends who kept checking in on where this book was at, every time you did, it spurred me on. And in advance to the friends who will buy a copy of this, thank you SO much. It means the world to me and is the greatest support to any author. To do just a little more to support me, I'd love it if you could leave a review!

To the amazing network of solo-preneur friends that I have, thank you so much for being a continual source of inspiration, for cheering me on in my (somewhat slow and sometimes random) journey of creativity and business.

To my family, thank you for your love and support, and your inevitable surprise about some of my stories.

Many thanks to Deb, Jane and Lesley, my health and wellbeing team who have taught me so much and supported me through some very difficult days, weeks, months, years.

And, to YOU, the reader. Thank you, it was always for you.

# Ways to work with Jade

There are a few ways you could work with me if you'd like to:

## WORKSHOPS and CONSULTING

My superpowers are simplifying complexity, visual thinking and strategic problem solving. I work with individuals and businesses about purpose, creativity, and communication. With over 20 years experience in communications, marketing, design, illustration, a neurodiverse brain, and now a published author, I bring a unique and personal approach to the work I do.

Much like the processes in this book, I use creative methods such as visual thinking and sketchnoting, to define business, values, mission and purpose, communicate it to your people, and align it with actions. I also work with individuals in coaching and goal setting to work towards a lemonade-loving life.

## SPEAKING

I am available to speak about topics in this book, or my broader work in communications and developing purpose led business. Please get in touch, I'd love to support you at your next event.

**Connect with me!**

hello@jademiller.com.au
Visit www.making-lemonade.com.au
I'm on LinkedIn at www.linkedin.com/jademillerconsulting
Find me on Instagram at www.instagram.com/lemonade_with_jade

www.ingramcontent.com/pod-product-compliance
Lightning Source LLC
Chambersburg PA
CBHW051428290426
**44109CB00016B/1477**